WHAT SUCCESSFUL COACHES ACROSS THE NATION ARE SAYING ABOUT CHAMPIONSHIP TEAM BUILDING. . .

"Championship Team Building helped us achieve one of the biggest turnarounds in basketball history. We went from a difficult 8-22 season to 22-10 and NCAA Elite 8 participants in one season. Several of the team enhancement, leadership, and Seven "C's" worked wonders and helped us achieve fun results, great chemistry, and better communication. Championship Team Building really works and I'll continue to highly recommend it to every coach!"

June Daugherty
Head Women's Basketball Coach
University of Washington
Pac-10 Champions 2001

"Jeff has created a coach's team building bible. It is a road map for any coach leading their team down the path to success and satisfaction. It's a must for any coach's library!!!"

Rhonda Revelle
Head Softball Coach
University of Nebraska
Big 12 Coach of the Year 1998

"Jeff's book reveals the secrets for building a championship team from the youth levels all the way to professional sports."

Angela Taylor
WNBA Coordinator of Player Personnel

"Championship Team Building should be required reading for all coaches. Jeff has put together an effective and easy to use resource covering all the great team building work he has done with our programs at Arizona and across the nation. It's the edge coaches need to build a winning program!"

Frank Busch
Head Men's & Women's Swimming Coach
University of Arizona
USA Swimming Coach of the Year 1998

CHAMPIONSHIP TEAM BUILDING

ADDITIONAL RESOURCES BY JEFF JANSSEN

Books

The Team Captain's Leadership Manual: The Complete Guide to Developing Team Leaders Whom Coaches Respect and Teammates Trust

The Seven Secrets of Successful Coaches: How to Unlock and Unleash Your Team's Full Potential

The Mental Makings of Champions: How to Win The Mental Game

Jeff Janssen's Peak Performance Playbook: 50 Drills, Activities & Ideas to Inspire Your Team, Build Mental Toughness & Improve Team Chemistry

Videos

Building a Winning Team Chemistry

Winning The Mental Game: How You Can Develop The Motivation, Confidence & Focus of Champions

Psychology of Sensational Hitting: How You Can Become a More Focused, Confident & Consistent Hitter with Leah O'Brien

Audio

The Softball Coach's Guide to Mental Training with Ken Ravizza

To order visit www.jeffjanssen.com or call toll free 1-888-721-TEAM.

CHAMPIONSHIP TEAM BUILDING

*What Every Coach Needs to Know
to Build a Motivated, Committed
& Cohesive Team*

Jeff Janssen

Winning The Mental Game
Cary, North Carolina

Published by Winning The Mental Game
102 Horne Creek Court, Cary, NC 27519
Phone: 1-888-721-TEAM
Fax: (919) 303-4338
Email: jeff@jeffjanssen.com
Website: www.jeffjanssen.com

Publisher's Cataloging-in-Publication
(Provided by Quality Books, Inc.)

Janssen, Jeff
    Championship team building : what every coach needs to
    know to build a motivated, committed & cohesive team /
    Jeff Janssen. -- 1st ed.
        p. cm.
        Includes bibliographical references and index.
        Preassigned LCCN: 98-90747
        ISBN: 1-892882-10-8

        1. Coaching (Athletics) 2. Teamwork (Sports)
    3. Leadership.   I. Title.

    GV711.J36 1999   796.07'7
                            QBI98-1272

Printed in the United States of America

10 9 8 7 6

DEDICATION

To Coach Mike Candrea

*Thanks for showing me what it takes to be
a champion both on and off the field.*

TABLE OF CONTENTS

Strategies and Solutions for Your Toughest Team Building Questions • What is Effective Team Building? • A Treasure Chest of Proven Team Building Ideas

Teams Do Not Succeed by Talent Alone • Talent Without Teamwork = Trouble • Success = Talent + Teamwork • Great Teamwork Must Be Taught and Developed • Benefits of Team Building • Team Building with Team & Individual Sports

Seven "C's" of Championship Team Building • How to Use this Book to Strengthen the Seven "C's" • Team Chemistry 101: The Stages of Team Development • Using the Stages of Team Development as You Coach • Common Problem Areas of Developing Your Team • Sailing the Seven "C's" With Your Team • Team Building Evaluation • Using Team Challenges and Games for Team Building
Team Building Challenge—The Human Knot

FOREWORD

Every coach agrees that team chemistry is absolutely critical to building a championship team. To be successful at any level of sport, you have to have players who respect each other and are willing to make personal sacrifices for the good of the team. As coaches, we constantly preach to our players about the importance of teamwork. We've all, at one time or another, used the old sayings, "There is no 'I' in team" and "TEAM means Together Everyone Achieves More" because we understand that great teamwork can help our team rise to a higher level. We know that when players come together, respect each other and work toward a common goal, that magical things can happen.

We also know that poor team chemistry causes us a lot of headaches and sleepless nights, not to mention lost games. We all have had seasons where we dreaded going to practice because our players refused to work together. It's not much fun coaching a selfish team when players only look out for themselves. It's extremely frustrating coaching a team when your players are not committed to excellence and consistently giving their best effort. It's also a miserable feeling when players are always talking about each other behind their backs and not getting along. The joy of coaching a team with great chemistry is matched only by the frustration of coaching a team with poor chemistry.

Knowing the importance of great team chemistry and the pain of poor team chemistry, it's amazing to me that there are so few resources available that coaches can use to help build their teams—until now.

Championship Team Building is the only book I know which provides coaches with a comprehensive plan for building a successful program. It's loaded with tried and true ideas and exercises to help you build great team chemistry. From the first page to the last, this book gives you an easy and workable blueprint to follow in building a championship program. How do I know the suggestions in this book work?

Because I've seen the power of these successful team building ideas first hand. Each year, Jeff does a variety of team building activities with our team. It culminates when we create a team building theme for our players before heading into the playoffs and the Women's College World Series. The theme does a great job of motivating, relaxing and unifying our team on our quest to perform at our best when it counts the most.

One powerful theme we used was for the 1996 Women's College World Series. We ended up second the previous year and entered the '96 season having lost five first-team All-Americans. While we still had a solid team returning, we did not have the most talented team in the tournament. Worse yet, heading into the final week of the season we weren't peaking the way I wanted us to be. At our last practice before Regionals, Jeff sat down with our team and told them a story.

It's a true story about a boy who grew up several years ago in Louisville, Kentucky. The boy's family was poor and they couldn't afford much more than the roof over his head. However, the other boys in the neighborhood all had bikes except for the boy. He would try to hang around with his friends but they would go riding off and as hard as he tried, he just couldn't keep up with them.

Knowing that his parents couldn't afford a bike, the boy decided to work for one himself. He found a job at a grocery store and after about a year's time, finally saved up enough money to buy his bike. He proudly bought the bike, rode home and showed it off to all his friends. It was the proudest day of his life because he had worked hard to earn his bike.

After about a week, the boy woke up one morning and went outside to where he had parked his bike—or thought he had parked his bike. Much to his surprise and shock, it was gone. Frantically, he asked all his friends, "Have you seen my bike?" Unfortunately none of them had. The boy was devastated because someone had stolen the bike that he had worked so hard to achieve.

Well, a few years later, the boy got involved in the sport of boxing. To motivate himself before stepping in the ring, the young man would look menacingly toward his opponent and say to himself, "Hey, that must be the guy who stole my bike!"

And Muhammed Ali ended up being a pretty good boxer in his time.

This story motivated and unified our players, for they understood that each time they took the field, they were on a mission to reclaim our stolen bike. It gave our team a common goal to rally around and we came out with a fire in our eyes for each and every game. The theme inspired us to play our best and helped us win the National Championship. On the inside of everyone's National Championship rings I had the words "Our Bike" inscribed. Our players pulled together, played with heart and reclaimed our bike.

For me, team building is one of the most challenging and exciting parts of coaching. Ironically, while I have been fortunate to coach some very talented athletes through the years, I probably enjoy the challenge of the seasons where we aren't necessarily the most talented team on paper. I really enjoy trying to put the different pieces of our team together so that we can perform as one by the end of the season. Jeff's outstanding work on team building has made a big difference with our team over the years and I know the ideas and suggestions in this book will be of great help to your team too. Best of luck!

Mike Candrea
Head Softball Coach
University of Arizona
NFCA Coach of the Year 1994, 96, 97
National Champions 1991, 93, 94, 96, 97, 2001

ACKNOWLEDGMENTS

Just as teamwork is critical to producing a championship team, so too is teamwork important in the creation of a book. While I am listed as the author, in actuality several people have given of themselves in the development of this book. I would like to take this opportunity to acknowledge the contributions they have made not only to this book but to my life as well.

I must begin by thanking all of the student-athletes whom I have been privileged to interact with through the years. I truly appreciate you opening up your minds and hearts to me and letting me share in your experiences as a college student-athlete. Because of you, I have yet to "work" a day in my life.

Thank you to the all the coaches I have played for, worked with, and observed. I have learned so much about championship team building from observing and interacting with you. I appreciate the trust you have in me by allowing me to work with your teams.

Thank you to my extended family of coaches and athletes around the world who have read my books, watched my videos and attended my seminars. Your interest and support of my work and that of my colleagues is a source of great inspiration for me.

Thank you to my mentors and colleagues in the in the field of mental training and team building, especially Ken Ravizza, Dave Yukelson, Greg Dale, Thad Leffingwell, Bob Harmison, Jean Williams and the members of Diego.

Special thanks to all the coaches, athletes and others who gave their insights on drafts of the book: Cami Banholzer, Gary Barnett, Becky Bell, Joan Bonvicini, Frank Busch, Mike Candrea, Greg Dale, Lisa Fraser, Jim Gault, Terri Mitchell, Ryk Neethling, David Odom, Josh Pastner, Jim Rosborough, Rhonda Revelle, John Rittman, Angela Taylor, Pat Williams and Dave Yukelson. I sincerely appreciate your comments and contributions.

Thanks to the many coaches who have shared their insights on what it takes to build a championship team through their books, videos and speeches. Coaches like Pat Summitt, Mike Krzyzewski, David Odom, Phil Jackson, Rick Pitino, Pat Riley, Gary Barnett, Pat Williams, Randy Brown, Red Auerbach, Vince Lombardi and Don Shula have had a tremendous impact on me. (This fact will become quite evident to you as you read many of their thoughts on championship team building throughout the book.) Even though I have not had the privilege of knowing some of you personally, you have been great mentors to me and I am forever grateful to you for giving me a glimpse of your philosophies and your teams.

Thank you to my parents, Tom and Mary Janssen, and sister Jaclyn. You have always believed in me and encouraged me to pursue my dreams. Without your love and support I'm not sure where I would be.

Thank you to my amazing children, Ryan and Jill. I'm so blessed to have you a part of the Janssen Team.

Finally, saving the best for last, thank you to my wife Kristi who is my best friend and teammate for life. Through our marriage you continually show me the power of what working together as a team can accomplish. While I am proud of the championship rings I am honored to have, the one I cherish the most is and always will be on my left ring finger.

INTRODUCTION

STRATEGIES AND SOLUTIONS FOR YOUR TOUGHEST TEAM BUILDING QUESTIONS

As a coach, you have probably found yourself searching for answers to these questions over the course of your coaching career:

How can I get my team to be just half as committed to success as I am?

How do I get everyone on the same page and focused on a common goal?

How do I convince my players to work together as a team?

How do I handle selfish players who have their own agendas?

How do I get my players to understand, appreciate and accept their roles?

How do I get my players to communicate better both on and off the court/field?

What can I do when my team has problems and can't get along with each other?

How can I get my players to be more responsible and accountable?

How can I get my team to respect and trust each other more?

If you're like most coaches, you have probably been confused, frustrated and even stumped by many of the above challenges that go into coaching a successful team. While there are hundreds of books, videos, clinics and other resources to help you overcome the physical, mechanical and tactical problems of your sport, there are very few resources available specifically written for coaches that you can use to build a more motivated, committed and cohesive team. Well, your search is over because this book will help you find answers for some of your toughest team building questions and problems. It will also provide you with a practical and proven guide that you can use to build a championship team.

WHAT IS EFFECTIVE TEAM BUILDING?

Team building is the process of planning, molding and guiding a group of individuals into a unified team. It is perhaps one of the most complicated and challenging, yet rewarding roles of coaching. As you probably already realize, successful team building actually requires coaches to have the skills and talents of many different occupations including salesperson, architect, firefighter, policeman, judge and jury, private detective, mediator and counselor. Effective coaching goes far beyond the mere teaching of sport skills and the positioning of bodies on the court or field. It also relies on the skillful blending of several individual dreams and fears into a collective and cohesive unit focused on a common goal.

Championship Team Building is designed to give you and your team a variety of ideas and strategies that you can use in the challenging, complex and dynamic process of team building. Each team and each new season is different, at least subtly, if not drastically because of the continual influx of new players, the departure of past players and the maturation of current players. Because your team is always evolving and changing, team building is a constant concern and challenge. Team building is an ongoing, complex process that is affected by a multitude of internal and external factors. Injuries, parents, roommates, weather, umpires, playing time, homesickness, transfers, trades and bad grades all have the potential to upset your team's chemistry without a moment's notice.

With eight years as the Peak Performance Coach for the University of Arizona athletic department and now as a consultant to many of the nation's top college teams, I have been fortunate to observe and be involved in over 200 different seasons of team building. Some of the teams bonded together to win National Championships while others suffered from selfishness and frustrating subpar seasons. While there is no one perfect way or set order of steps you can take to automatically guarantee that everyone will "love, honor and cherish each other 'til the end of the season do they part," there are several things you can do to create an effective team atmosphere focused on success.

The following pages contain a number of the ideas, strategies and solutions which I have found effective with many different teams across a variety of sports. I am confident that these strategies will work for you and your team as well, no matter what level you coach. While all of them have been used and tested in the real world, I want to stress that never before has every single one of them been used with one team during the same season—it would be absolute overload.

A TREASURE CHEST OF PROVEN TEAM BUILDING IDEAS

What I want to provide you with is a treasure chest of proven team building ideas at your fingertips. The best coaches I know constantly search for new ideas that could make a difference with their team. My bet is that there is at least one if not dozens of ideas in these pages that will enhance your team's success and satisfaction. Your job is to modify and extend these ideas and strategies to fit your unique situation.

I have been extremely fortunate to sail the sometimes turbulent seas of team building many times and hope to serve as a guide on your exciting journey. By taking an in depth look at the championship team building experiences of some of the world's greatest coaches, athletes and teams, you will gain tremendous insights into what it takes to build a winning team. You will learn how to successfully battle many of the obstacles and adversities that have kept teams from reaching their full potential and getting to their desired destinations. You will also learn many of the routes and occasional trade winds that lead to the promised land. Thanks for letting me come along on your team's championship journey to greater success and satisfaction!

CHAPTER 1

THE IMPORTANCE OF TEAMWORK

Why You Need to Build Your Team

TEAMS DO NOT SUCCEED BY TALENT ALONE

Understandably, coaches across the world spend a great deal of their time searching for and developing talent. They spend countless hours discovering and evaluating the most talented players to draft and recruit. Then, when they get them on their team, they spend even more time trying to develop and refine their physical ability. Physical talent in sport is undeniably important, however, talent alone does not equal success.

To prove that talent is not the only key to winning, simply ask yourself, "Does the most talented team always win the championship?" Definitely not! If that were the case, there would be no need to play out your season because after evaluating who the most talented team was on paper, the championship could be awarded. Perhaps the aspect that draws many coaches and athletes to sport is the fact that success requires more than physical talent. Success also requires teamwork.

> *"You're not going to win with the kids who are just All-Americans. The kids must have more than status, they must have togetherness."*
> —Coach John Thompson, Georgetown University men's basketball

Talent Without Teamwork = Trouble

Every season there are numerous examples of teams that have all the right talent to compete for the championship but end up losing and falling painfully short of their goals. Occasionally it is bad luck or an off day, but more often than not it is due to a lack of teamwork.

There are several powerful forces that can keep your team from achieving its true potential. Sadly, these forces are not always your opponents but, ironically, are sometimes your own players. Internal problems like selfishness, jealousies, poor communication, conflict and a lack of commitment to a common goal have kept just as many teams from winning championships as have more talented opponents. Despite their talent, players with personal agendas can sabotage all the hard work you have invested in your season. Conflict within your team can take your focus away from your goals and drain the energy and motivation from your players. A lack of commitment to working hard and putting in quality practices can keep your talent from ever achieving its full potential.

One of our goals on our journey through this book is to recognize and minimize the destructive forces which often distract, disrupt and divide teams. By identifying and understanding the problems that can arise within your team, we can proactively and effectively prevent your players from working against each other and undermining your team's success.

"There are plenty of teams in every sport that have great players and will never win titles. Most times those players aren't willing to sacrifice for the greater good of the team. The funny thing is, in the end, their unwillingness to sacrifice only makes individual goals more difficult to achieve."
—Michael Jordan, Chicago Bulls/Washington Wizards

"A great collection of talent with unbalanced chemistry and inappropriate attitudes can get knocked over by teams of lesser talent."
—Coach Pat Riley, Miami Heat

Success = Talent + Teamwork

The occasionally frustrating yet exciting and challenging aspect of sport is that success requires a combination of both talent and teamwork. Teamwork is the necessary and important ingredient which allows your talent to work together in harmony. When your team is unified toward a common cause and willing to give it their all for the good of the team, your success is enhanced exponentially and magical things can happen. Teamwork somehow has the power to take your team to another, often unexpected level. It has the special ability of making 2+2 = 5, or 6, or even 10.

While you would likely prefer to have the most talented team heading into the season, there are countless examples of teams who have won championships with only solid talent but spectacular teamwork. Thus, teamwork is important regardless of your talent level. If your talent level isn't the best, you need teamwork to give you the extra edge to compete with the more talented teams. And if you have the "horses," teamwork is necessary to get and keep them on the same page so they can work together and perform to their potential. As most championship coaches and athletes have discovered, teamwork is often the critical ingredient of success that transcends the power of talent.

> *"Attitude and chemistry are the factors that control winning,*
> *no matter what the talent level."*
> —Coach Gary Barnett, University of Colorado football

> *"Talent wins games, but teamwork and*
> *intelligence win championships."*
> —Michael Jordan, Chicago Bulls/Washington Wizards

> *"This championship was special because of the way*
> *we had to go about winning. I think it was a true test*
> *of our character, our heart, our togetherness."*
> —Coach Mike Candrea, University of Arizona softball

Our other major goal will be to identify the characteristics of successful teams which allow them to rise to championship levels. We will examine the characteristics of championship teams and show you how to build and strengthen them within your team.

GREAT TEAMWORK MUST BE TAUGHT AND DEVELOPED

While many coaches spend a great deal of their time finding and developing the talent part of the equation through their recruiting, practices, weights and conditioning workouts, take a moment to consider how much of your time is invested in team building? Because teamwork is critical to your team's success, it is important to invest the time in developing it, just as you spend time developing your talent.

> *". . . Teamwork is taught. You don't just lump a group of people together in a room and call them a team and expect them to behave like one."*
> —Coach Pat Summitt, University of Tennessee women's basketball

> *"It's easy to find great players. What's hard is getting people to play as a team. That's the selling job."*
> —Coach Chuck Daly, USA Basketball

Benefits of Team Building

Team building benefits your team in a multitude of ways. The two most prominent ones are greater success and satisfaction.

1. Success

Effective team building will help you and your team achieve greater levels of success. It enhances your team's success by maximizing your potential while minimizing internal problems. Team building maximizes your potential by focusing your team's efforts toward achieving a common goal.

Team building also enhances your success by minimizing the divisive internal problems that can distract and destroy your team. When we examine the model below, we can see that effective teams spend the majority of their energy externally, focusing on and working toward their common goal. They devote roughly 90% of their time and energy productively pursuing their goals. Moderately effective teams spend roughly half their time focused on their goals and the other half trying to overcome internal problems. Ineffective teams spend the majority of their time dealing with internal problems and conflict, which leaves little time to focus on their goals.

Effective Team   **Moderately Effective**   **Ineffective Team**

2. Satisfaction

Not only will an effective team greatly increase your odds of winning, but equally as important, team building will make the entire sport experience much more enjoyable for you and your players. While the majority of coaches and athletes get involved in sport for the challenge and joy of winning, a sense of satisfaction from the close relationships which you and your players develop is often an unmentioned, yet important reward of the team building process.

Can you think of a single coach who would not want increased success and satisfaction for themselves and their team? While you should continue your efforts of finding and developing talent, it is also important for you to invest some time in championship team building—which is probably why you bought this book! As you will soon see, the benefits of investing time in building a championship team will be more than worth your while.

TEAM BUILDING WITH TEAM AND INDIVIDUAL SPORTS

Obviously, team building is an important aspect in team sports like basketball, football, softball, baseball, soccer, volleyball, hockey, etc. Classified as interacting sports, these sports rely on a smooth and synergistic interaction between teammates to be successful. Football teams rely on 11 players to advance the ball across the goal line and another 11 to prevent their opponents from doing so. Basketball teams rely on five players to pass the ball and set screens which lead to high percentage shots. Baseball and softball teams depend on nine players to catch and throw the ball without letting baserunners get on or advance. Without a common goal and a cohesive team, success would be nearly impossible to achieve. Thus, it is easy to see why teamwork is vital to the success of interacting teams.

What about individual sports like tennis, golf, track, swimming and gymnastics where the individual athlete's performance does not necessarily depend on that of a teammate? Is team building still important for these teams? If you coach one of these sports I'm expecting to hear a resounding "YES!" Although the players of these sports do not have to interact with each other much when competing, they often need to interact with each other outside of actual competition. Throughout the course of a season, they will spend more time working together as a team during practices, weights, conditioning and mental training than they will within competition. Furthermore, commitment to a common goal, clear communication, constructive conflict and even cohesion still are critical areas to the success and satisfaction of these teams.

Ironically, individual, or co-acting sports as they are sometimes called, usually require a greater emphasis on teamwork when they start competing within a team setting. Why? Because the team concept is foreign to many individual sport athletes since they often train and compete on their own. They become accustomed to getting all of their coach's attention, working out when they want to and focusing only on their wants, needs and goals. This environment has a tendency to create self-centered and spoiled athletes.

However, when they are brought into a team setting, individual sport athletes often don't know how to react. Now they need to share a coach's time with their teammates. They need to wait until a teammate is finished with her drills and repetitions. They need to play a role instead of being the center of attention. And finally, they have to sacrifice some of their personal goals for the good of the team. Sadly, for some individual sport athletes, their first exposure to being part of a team doesn't occur until they get to college. Thus, many times I spend a lot of my time working with the individual sport athletes (gymnasts, tennis players, golfers) who now need to learn how to work together as a team.

Thus, it really doesn't matter whether you coach a team or individual sport, successful team building is a big key to your team's success.

INTRODUCTION SUMMARY
TEAM BUILDING TIPS

- Remember, success is more than talent—it also requires teamwork.

- Teamwork does not happen automatically but must be developed over time.

- Team building maximizes your team's potential by getting your talent to work together.

- Team building minimizes the internal problems that can distract, divide and destroy your team.

- Along with greater success, team building also enhances your team's sense of satisfaction.

- Team building is important for both team and individual sports.

CHAPTER 2

THE SEVEN "C's" OF CHAMPIONSHIP TEAM BUILDING

Common Characteristics of Championship Teams

Before we jump into how to build a successful team, it is important to have a clear understanding of the characteristics of championship teams as well as how teams typically develop. As I've already mentioned, some degree of physical talent is important and necessary in building a championship team. Obviously, you need talented athletes to compete. However, the point to keep in mind is that the team with the most talent does not always win the game. This is where teamwork comes into play.

The championship teams that I have been privileged to work with have had many important characteristics in common. I like to call them the Seven "C's" of Championship Team Building. It doesn't matter what sport, level or gender you coach, these seven characteristics produce championship teams.

SEVEN "C's" OF CHAMPIONSHIP TEAM BUILDING

1. Common Goal

Championship teams have a singular, common focus. The team is most often focused on winning a conference and/or National Championship.

13

This is their primary, specified, overt goal and all other goals revolve around it. All the members of the team, coaching staff and support staff fully support and embrace the goal. Everyone understands that this is the direction and destination the team is moving toward. Additionally, the goal the team is striving for typically is so challenging that the only way it can be accomplished is through a unified effort.

2. Commitment

While seasons may start with the entire team focused on a common goal, they rarely end up that way. Commitment is probably the single most important factor that differentiates championship teams, coaches, athletes, businesses, schools, marriages (you name it) from the mediocre. It's much too easy to say you want to win the championship and it's a whole other thing to put in the blood, sweat and tears necessary to pursue a championship—especially when obstacles and adversities strike. Continual commitment to the team's common goal is one of the toughest areas of team building.

Championship teams buy into the mission at every level and make it their own. They work hard and pay their dues because they want to, not because they have to. In addition to their commitment, the team members feel a sense of personal and group accountability. The players have a clear understanding of how their individual choices and decisions influence the collective psyche and success of the team. There is a true sense that if an individual is slacking off, he is not just hurting himself but his entire team. The players feel a sense of responsibility and obligation to give it their best.

3. Complementary Roles

Championship teams are comprised of several individuals who willingly take pride in playing specific roles. These roles, when played in concert and harmony, lead to team success. Thus, each player is assigned specific responsibilities and tasks that determine the entire team's success. While individually they are not solely responsible for the team's success or failure, collectively each role forms a synergistic whole which is greater than the sum of its parts.

The major difficulty in developing complementary roles is that some roles get more attention and praise, thereby making them seem more important. Championship teams however, realize that all roles are critical to the overall team's success and willingly accept and value their individual roles.

4. Clear Communication

A fourth characteristic of championship teams is clear communication. Coaches and players clearly communicate with each other in an open and honest manner. They communicate on a frequent basis, discussing their goals, strategies, successes and concerns. Championship teams communicate successfully both on and off the field/court. The on field communication helps them perform more efficiently in competition. The off field communication allows them to monitor the team's effectiveness, modify things when necessary and celebrate successes.

5. Constructive Conflict

Along with effective communication, championship teams have the ability to keep conflict under control and often use it constructively to further develop and strengthen the team. It is not that championship teams never experience conflict, because this is impossible. Instead, they effectively handle the conflict that arises and do not let it interfere with the team's common goal.

6. Cohesion

A sixth characteristic shared by many championship teams is that the players genuinely like and respect each other. Many championship teams will spend a great deal of time socializing together in larger groups outside of scheduled practice and game times. They find reasons to stay together like going to the movies, studying, hanging out, etc. This is not to say that every single player is a part of the group, but that a majority of players tend to socialize together. Cohesion means that the players generally enjoy each other's company and treat their teammates with respect.

7. Credible Coaching

Finally, it takes a credible coach to develop, orchestrate and monitor all the other "C's" of Championship Team Building. The team must have a leader who they believe in and has the skills necessary to get the most out of them. A credible coach creates an environment which allows the team to perform to its fullest potential. While the aspects of credible coaching deserve an entire book to do the topic justice, the team building skills you will learn in this book will certainly enhance your credibility as a coach.

The Seven "C's" of Championship Team Building are the core characteristics of championship teams. Whether you coach a youth baseball team, a junior high girls soccer team, a high school football team, a junior college volleyball team, a college gymnastics team or a WNBA basketball team, these seven characteristics are the key to your success. Without these critical characteristics, your team will never achieve its true potential, no matter how talented your players might be.

How to Use this Book to Strengthen the Seven "C's"

This book is filled with practical and proven strategies to help you develop the Seven "C's" of Championship Team Building. The following chapters of the book provide an in depth look at each of the Seven "C's" so you can build and strengthen the characteristics within your team. While they are distinct characteristics, you will find that they are also highly interrelated. Thus, I recommend you read the book all the way through to see how the concepts fit together and build upon each other.

However, if you are pressed for time (as most coaches are), you can also take the Team Building Evaluation located within this chapter and then go directly to the specific chapter(s) you feel your team would benefit from the most. Further, after reading through it the first time, you can continue to use the book throughout your coaching career as a quick reference and resource guide in the ever-changing and ever-challenging process of team building.

TEAM CHEMISTRY 101: THE STAGES OF TEAM DEVELOPMENT

Before we begin the team building process, it is important to understand the ways in which teams tend to develop. Team building is a process which often unfolds over time. You will likely encounter certain stages in team building complete with barriers and breakthroughs.

According to Tuckman (1965), group development tends to progress in a certain order. To gain a better understanding of the typical stages of team development, let's explore how his model relates to your team. By examining some common stages through which the majority of teams must pass, this model gives you a better feel for what to expect and how to coach your team accordingly.

> *"There are common challenges that every team, and every team player, must conquer on their road to significant achievement."*
> —Coach Pat Riley, Miami Heat

1. Forming

For most teams, each new season begins with the Forming stage. One of your first steps as coach is to determine the composition of your team. You are continually adding people through recruiting, transfers, trades and tryouts as well as subtracting people from your team through graduation, retirement and injuries. Your coaching and support staff also undergo many changes over the years and these differences have an impact on the makeup and character of your team. In some minor or major way, your team is altered and influenced each time a member is added or subtracted.

The Forming stage begins with your first meeting or practice and is characterized by the individuals getting to know each other. This stage involves a great deal of uneasiness and uncertainty because some team members are not even sure if they will make the final team. Others know they will make the team but are unsure about the role they might play. Experienced players will be trying to get a feel for the newcomers in an attempt to see if they can help the team or if their position might be threatened. On the surface, most people will be cordial and friendly as they meet and interact with their new teammates, but internally there are often a lot of unanswered questions that can cause doubt and stress. Chapter Nine on Cohesion offers some suggestions to help you and your team get to know each other better during the Forming stage.

2. Storming

The second stage occurs when a group of individuals with various wants, needs and insecurities starts to more closely interact and compete with one another. The Storming stage usually occurs a few weeks into your season. Inevitably, because of the various personalities and goals on your team, conflicts between players, coaches and staff will arise. Players will test your standards as a coach just as you will test theirs. Individuals will be overtly and covertly vying for starting positions and leadership roles. Poor work ethics and bad attitudes will be exposed. Your team will quickly discover who will be playing what positions and roles as well as how much playing time each person will get. Remember, each player enters the season with a certain set of expectations of how things should be for them individually and for the rest of the team. Naturally conflict arises when the expectations and desires of various individuals come into contact.

What many coaches do not fully understand and appreciate is that the Storming stage is a necessary and important stage of team development. Your goal as a coach is not to prevent conflict from happening, which is impossible, but to handle and channel conflict into effective individual and team development. Your attitude and approach to conflict is a crucial variable in successful team building as you will learn throughout this book. You may even want to alert your team to the fact that not everyone is going to agree with and like each other 100% of the time and that this is a normal part of team development. The biggest key is how your team handles the inevitable conflict. Chapters Seven and Eight on Clear Communication and Constructive Conflict are dedicated to strategies to help your team effectively communicate and keep conflict under control.

FOUR STAGES OF TEAM DEVELOPMENT

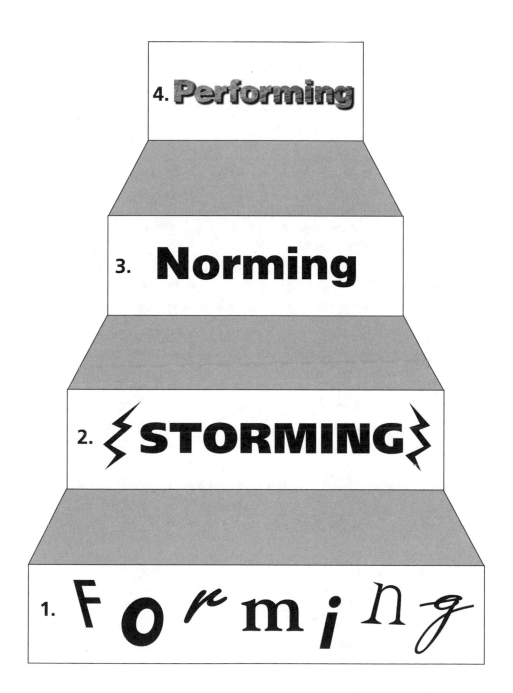

3. Norming

The Norming stage occurs when the team begins to settle on a set of rules and standards as to how things will be done. Norming relates to your team's standards in practice, the classroom, weight training, conditioning, mental training, social life, etc. Occasionally, these standards are formally written and agreed upon but typically they evolve over time as "this is the way we do things."

Obviously, your team's norms, standards and rules concerning their attitude, work ethic, team support, etc. have a tremendous impact on the success of your team. As a coach, it is important that your team norms create and foster a successful environment. Unfortunately, the norms in too many teams across the nation reflect many businesses across America. Many struggling businesses live by the norms of "Do just enough to get by," and "Thank God it's Friday."

Chapters Three through Five on Common Goal, Commitment, and Committing to a Common Goal will give you and your team the tools to create effective standards as well as a system to monitor how well your team is working together.

4. Performing

The Performing stage is the eventual goal of all teams. This stage follows the Norming stage and occurs only if effective standards are in place and firmly embraced by the team. In the Performing stage the team begins performing as a confident and cohesive unit. The players feel a sense of comfort, consistency and trust because they know what to expect from each other. Coaches talk a lot about peaking at the end of the season. The Performing stage is exactly the "peaking" that all coaches covet—when the team is jelling and working together like a well-oiled machine.

Unfortunately, the Performing stage is not a guaranteed aspect of your season. Performing requires that your team has constructively handled the conflict of the Storming stage. Not only do you need to overcome the conflict, but you and your team must also establish effective rules and standards in the Norming stage to ascend to the Performing stage.

> *"Coming together is a beginning,*
> *Keeping together is progress,*
> *Working together is success."*
> —Henry Ford

Using the Stages of Team Development as You Coach

Your job as coach is to use the stages of team development as a guide to facilitate your team's natural progression through these stages. Remember, not all teams will automatically progress sequentially through these stages, but this model will serve as a good guide for your team's development. Problems arise when coaches are not familiar with the stages of team development or when they try to push a team to the Performing stage too soon.

Teams can go back and forth between these stages, especially as new challenges and demands arise throughout the season. Injuries, conflicts and losses can cause a team to regress from the Norming stage back into the Storming stage. As I've mentioned, team building is a complex, ever-changing process that must be continually monitored and adjusted.

> *"I realized that the team would take time to evolve into a*
> *cohesive whole. My challenge was to be patient. There's no*
> *percentage in trying to push the river or speed the harvest."*
> —Coach Phil Jackson, Los Angeles Lakers

Common Problem Areas of Developing Your Team
1. Stuck in the Storming Stage

Keeping these stages in mind, most of the problems I see with teams are ones of conflict where teams get stuck in the Storming stage. Conflicts continually flare up because individuals often do not have the skills and/or maturity to effectively handle their differences. These differences are either perpetual open sores, or they are swept under the carpet only to fester and rear their ugly heads at the most disastrous times. The Constructive Conflict Chapter is designed to give you and your team the necessary tools and strategies to effectively move through the Storming stage.

2. Negative Norms

Additionally, some teams make their way through the Storming stage but their unproductive norms become their eventual downfall. If you're not careful your team's standards may be totally counterproductive to your success. "Do enough to get by, Every person for themselves, Coach plays favorites," are all norms and attitudes which could prevent your team from reaching its full potential.

Teams with poor standards continually keep themselves from progressing. In this situation, coaches often intentionally shake up their teams and move them back into the Storming stage. This happens when you challenge their attitudes, work ethics and standards because you recognize that they are actually hurting the team. Your goal is to get them to recognize their behavior and how it runs counter to the goals they have set. Then you need to encourage and help them establish more effective standards—or sometimes even impose more effective standards.

SAILING THE SEVEN "C's" WITH YOUR TEAM

Discovering Your Secret Formula for Team Chemistry

Since we have discussed the goals and benefits of team building, the characteristics of championship teams and the typical stages of team development, it is now time to begin formulating an effective plan so you can build a more motivated, committed and cohesive team. This plan is organized to help you implement the characteristics of an effective team while considering the stages of development. Use this formula as a framework to support your team building as you respect the uniqueness of your team. I strongly encourage you to use what you believe will be the most effective and feel free to adapt the suggestions and exercises in the book to fit your team's specific needs. Remember, there is no perfect way to build a successful team. As is much of coaching, a lot of team building is based on acquiring and trusting a certain feel or intuition you have for what is right for your team in any given situation.

The basic framework for determining your formula for championship team building involves the following four steps:

1. Assess
2. Strategize
3. Implement
4. Evaluate

Assess the Entire Situation

The first key to team building is to assess as much information about the team as possible. Yes, this does sound like a lot of work but most coaches who have been around their teams have discovered and stored much of this information already. Coaches taking a new job or first time coaches will have to do more research.

As the season and your coaching career progresses, you will begin to understand a lot more about the history, environment and dynamics surrounding your team. In essence, you must gather a detailed scouting report on your own team. Remember that knowledge is power—the more you know on the front end, the better equipped you will be to handle situations appropriately.

For example, business man Harvey Mackay has written some excellent books including *Swim with the Sharks without Being Eaten Alive,* which have definite application to the coaching field. Before Mackay even meets with a prospective client he does his homework and finds out as much as he can about the prospect and his company. He goes so far as completing the Mackay 66—which is a series of 66 questions about the prospect's business, family life and community involvement before an initial meeting with a prospect. By doing this, Mackay gains a complete understanding of the situation he faces before trying to make the sale. Similarly, you too must have a comprehensive understanding of the dynamics of your team before you begin. In team building, what you don't know ahead of time can come back to hurt and haunt you!

Here are some of the things I like to know about a team before working with them:

1. **Past records**—both recent and long term history. Is this a team that has never won a conference championship in the history of the program or has this team won last year's state championship?

2. **Team Leaders**—Who are the team leaders, both positively and negatively?

3. **Influential People**—Who are the other people that influence the team (trainers, managers, strength coach)?

4. **Player Backgrounds**—What kind of family and socioeconomic backgrounds have the players come from?

5. **Relationships**—Who likes and dislikes whom?

6. **Experience**—Is this a senior-laden, veteran team or are there several newcomers/freshmen? How many of the players are returning starters and will there be much competition for spots?

7. **Coach's Credibility**—Do the players trust and respect the coach?

Involve Your Staff to Accurately Assess Your Team

Before your season begins, sit down with your staff and assess the status of your team. Take an honest and complete inventory. List your strengths and areas for improvement. List the biggest obstacles which could keep your team from being successful. List the most important keys to your team's success this season. List your team leaders. Then if you have a group of returning players, take an inventory of each team member in a similar way—strengths, limitations, obstacles, keys to coaching and handling.

Based on these assessments, what would you consider to be a successful season? For many coaches this automatically means wins and losses. In essence, you are looking at your situation and trying to set some challenging yet realistic goals and expectations for your season. Usually this process occurs sometime following the previous season. Share the experience with your staff and openly discuss everyone's insights and input.

Rate Your Team

A more formal and comprehensive way to evaluate your team can be done by using a written evaluation. An example of a written evaluation can be found on the following page with the Team Building Evaluation. You can use it in a variety of ways to help you better assess the inner workings of your team.

Take a moment to rate your team on each of the Seven "C's" of Championship Team Building using the Team Building Evaluation. If you are reading this book while you are in season, you should be able to answer all of the questions. However, if you are between seasons or just at the beginning of your year, it might be difficult for you to adequately rate some of the questions at this time. You can either rate last year's team or wait until you are at least two to three weeks into your season so that you can better evaluate your team. After completing the evaluation, see how you and your team fared using the Rating Scale.

Have Your Players Rate the Team

Additionally, the Team Building Evaluation is designed to be used with your players as well. I suggest you have your players fill out the evaluation anonymously so that you can more accurately assess what is going on with the team. Having your team fill out the evaluation should provide you with some tremendous insights. Your players may confirm your beliefs in some sections and surprise you in a few others. When used with your players, the evaluation will not only tap into their viewpoints, but also serves as a good catalyst for discussion and launching your team building program.

TEAM BUILDING EVALUATION

This evaluation is designed to help you analyze the strengths and areas of improvement of your team. Please read each question and circle your response according to the scale below.

1 = Strongly Disagree   2 = Disagree   3 = Agree   4 = Strongly Agree

SD D A SA

Common Goal

1. The team has established a clear and compelling goal to pursue for the season   1 2 3 4
2. I am confident this team has the talent and ability to achieve the season goal   1 2 3 4
3. The standards and rules we have set for the team will help us achieve our goals   1 2 3 4
4. Everyone on the team is working toward the same team goal   1 2 3 4

Total _____

Commitment

5. The team has a strong work ethic, we have few players who slack off   1 2 3 4
6. The team often has players who come early to practices and stay late for extra work   1 2 3 4
7. The team's success is a high priority for most players   1 2 3 4
8. The team persists through most obstacles and adversities that come our way   1 2 3 4

Total _____

Complementary Roles

9. Players on this team clearly understand the roles they need to play for team success   1 2 3 4
10. Coaches and players show appreciation for all of the roles on our team, including the subs   1 2 3 4
11. Most players on this team have accepted their roles and are willing to play them   1 2 3 4
12. Players on the team are willing to sacrifice their individual goals for the good of the team   1 2 3 4

Total _____

Communication

13. Communication between the coaches and players is honest, clear and effective   1 2 3 4
14. Communication among players is honest, clear and effective   1 2 3 4
15. The team communicates effectively during competition   1 2 3 4
16. Coaches and players listen well to each other's opinions and feelings   1 2 3 4

Total _____

Constructive Conflict

17. This team does a good job of constructively addressing conflict when it arises   1 2 3 4
18. Players on the team generally can tolerate each other's minor differences   1 2 3 4
19. Team members respect each other and seldom talk about teammates behind their backs   1 2 3 4
20. Players on the team do not take personal conflicts on the field/court when they play   1 2 3 4

Total _____

Cohesion

21. Players on the team like to hang out with each other outside of games and practices   1 2 3 4
22. Players on the team generally respect and trust each other   1 2 3 4
23. Players on this team stick up for each other when criticized from the outside   1 2 3 4
24. Players on this team help and take care of each other when teammates are struggling   1 2 3 4

Total _____

Credible Coaching

25. The players believe in the coach(es) as a credible, competent and caring leader(s)   1 2 3 4
26. The coach(es) generally has a good feel for what is going on with our team   1 2 3 4
27. There is good, solid and positive leadership from the players/captains on this team   1 2 3 4
28. The coach(es) creates a positive and productive environment to help us reach our goals   1 2 3 4

Total _____

When you are finished, add up the score for each section. Then add the totals of the seven sections together to get your Total Score on the Team Building Evaluation.

TOTAL SCORE [   ]

TEAM BUILDING EVALUATION RATING SCALE

TOTAL

SCORE	Rating	Comments
98—112	Great	Congratulations! Your team is functioning at a very high level.
84—97	Good	Overall your team is doing well, a few improvements should help.
70—83	Okay	While your team is okay, improving it should enhance your success.
56—69	Poor	Your team is struggling and you should invest time to improve it.
42—55	Terrible	You've got some serious work to do to improve your team.
Below 42	Chaos	Consider finding another team (or another job).

Section Scores

14—16	Great
11- 13	Good
10	Okay
7—9	Poor
4—6	Terrible

Notice which areas you perceive as strengths and which areas need improvement. No matter where you ranked yourself presently, remember that your team chemistry is highly likely to fluctuate throughout the season. Thus, if you gave yourself a favorable rating now, be careful not to get overconfident and think your team has it made. You need to continually monitor your team throughout the season. For those of you who gave your team lower ratings, regardless of how bad it seems right now, there is hope. (Although sometimes it is hoping for next year to get here soon!) After all, by reading this book you have shown the commitment necessary to get your team on track. As you turn the pages, look for ideas you can use and adapt in an effort to improve your weaknesses.

The Team Building Evaluation is a tool you can use throughout your season to monitor the effectiveness of your team. I encourage you to use it on a regular basis—monthly probably works best. Praise your team for the things they are doing well and discuss ways to improve your lower rated areas. The evaluation will help you and your players effectively monitor the vital signs of your team.

Strategize

After thoroughly assessing your team, the next step is to come up with some effective ways to maintain your strengths and improve your weaknesses. Again, discussing this with your staff, support staff and/or other coaching colleagues is a great way to get various insights and ideas. Of course, the rest of the book will provide you with many options you can use for strengthening each of the Seven "C's" of Championship Team Building.

Using Team Challenges and Games for Team Building

One of the best ways to have your team learn about the importance of team building is through actually experiencing it. Some years ago a colleague of mine named Jerry Jerome introduced me to the benefits of adventure-based, experiential exercises for team building. Out of the many memorable, meaningful and fun experiences I have had working with teams, the team building challenges and games are definitely some of the highlights—and the ones players and coaches remember best!

Team building challenges and games allow your players to actually experience the demands and rewards of being a successful team. Some of you may have experienced team building through high elements, commercial Ropes Courses, but the ones I often use are short, simple and much more economical. Whether you use a Ropes Course or the exercises listed in this book, the challenges offer a fun and enlightening way to help you and your team learn what it takes to work together. They can be used with teams ranging from age five to age 95, although some exercises tend to be more active than others. Typically they are based around activities that require teamwork and highlight many of the Seven "C's" of Championship Team Building.

Some of the activities focus on having a common goal, others on role playing, communication, problem-solving, conflict management, accountability and trust, and many a combination of these skills. The activities often symbolize the demands and challenges that your team will face throughout the season, just compressed into a time frame anywhere from a minute to an hour. The activities and challenges help you as a coach learn a lot about your team, such as who the leaders are, how your players communicate and interact under pressure and how they handle obstacles and adversity. Additionally, your players gain insights on the team as a whole as well as learn a lot about themselves as part of the process. Project Adventure has some excellent resources on experiential games and I have listed their books in the Recommended Readings section in the back.

Not Just Fun and Games

One of the key areas for using team challenges and games is not the activities themselves, but the processing of the team concepts generated by the games. While they can be a lot of fun, the best way to use the activities is to learn something from them that will create a lasting impression on your players. Thus, you need to take the time to effectively discuss what the team learned and gained from the activities, and more importantly, how the team plans to act on these insights throughout the season. I encourage and challenge you to use the long term benefits of team building games rather than stopping at the short term fun.

Interestingly, the processing and discussion of the exercises is actually the most complicated and important aspect of using team games. To gain lasting benefits from the team challenges, you need to skillfully process and discuss the experience. A skilled facilitator can promote awareness and insights that will give your players a better understanding of successful teams as well as their team in particular. This requires a leader who is experienced in planning the games, overseeing their use in a *safe*, enjoyable and effective manner, facilitating and focusing a discussion of the games, and bridging the gap between using the games for fun and creating lasting attitudes and actions that will guide your team throughout the season.

While you could lead many of the team challenges and subsequent discussion, I strongly recommend you enlist the assistance of an experienced facilitator. The facilitator will ensure that you and your team get the most out of your team building challenges and conduct them in a safe manner. The majority of the team challenges are not very dangerous. However, like practice, injuries can happen any time you have a group of people engaged in physical activities. *Always emphasize safety with your players.*

Additionally, your opinion of your players is of great concern to them. Thus, what they say and don't say might be influenced by your presence. If you are planning to lead the team discussion, you must remember to be open to your team's ideas and input without imposing your own beliefs on them at this early stage. I have seen coaches begin to discuss things with their teams but then quickly turn the discussion into a one-sided lecture. Therefore, I recommend using an experienced outside group leader if at all possible. They will have the skills necessary to oversee the team building activities and facilitate the important discussion and lessons necessary to gain insights into your team.

As you go through the chapters highlighting each of the Seven "C's," I have included some examples of simple team challenges you can use to help your team experience teamwork at the end of each chapter. These exercises are some of the initial, basic ones that I use. If you are looking for additional, more advanced exercises, please see the Recommended Readings section at the end of the book which includes several excellent resources. (Or feel free to contact me at 1-888-721-TEAM for more information on the Championship Team Building Workshops I offer.)

Implement

After assessing your team and strategizing some possible ways to improve your weaknesses, the third step is simply to implement your plan. Decide on which strategy you are going to use, whether it is an activity, game or discussion, and do it.

Evaluate

As you implement your strategy, take the time to evaluate its effectiveness. Decide whether or not you achieved your objective and if this was something to which your team responded favorably. You can either ask your players what they thought about the team building or have them fill out a short evaluation on it afterwards. Several team building suggestions are listed throughout the rest of the chapters so if at first you don't succeed, there are many more ideas you can use.

CHAPTER TWO SUMMARY
TEAM BUILDING TIPS

- The Seven "C's" of Championship Team Building are critical to your team's success.

- All teams tend to progress through various stages of development during the season.

- Teams need time to get acquainted with each other when they first form.

- Conflict is a normal part of team development and needs to be handled constructively.

- The standards a team sets and lives by largely determines its overall success.

- Teams need to successfully progress through all stages to peak at the end of the season.

- The coach's job is to help guide the team through each of the stages.

- Teams can get stuck when they are unable to resolve conflict effectively.

- Teams can get stuck when they live by ineffective standards.

- Coaches should carefully assess their teams and devise an action plan to improve.

- Team challenges are a fun and effective way to introduce team concepts and initiate discussion.

References
Mackay, H. (1988). *Swim with the sharks without being eaten alive.* New York: Ivy Books.
Tuckman, B.W. (1965). Development sequence in small groups. *Psychological Bulletin, 63,* 384-399.

Team Building Challenge—The Human Knot

Objective
One of the most simple and effective team challenges to use is what is commonly called the Human Knot. The typically brief exercise powerfully communicates the importance of the Seven "C's" of Championship Team Building. I often use the challenge to kickoff team building when I work with teams because it is so easy and effective.

Setup
The human knot exercise requires an even number of people to accomplish. You need at least six people to do the exercise. Six can complete it relatively quickly and easily, eight to ten people makes it more difficult and a bit longer, and twelve and above can be a real challenge. Thus, if you have a team of 12 or more people I recommend you break them up into groups of roughly six when you first begin. You can always make it more challenging later once they get the hang of it.

Instructions
Have the even-numbered group(s) form a small circle. Instruct them to raise their right hand. Have them join hands with a person who is standing across from them. Then have them raise their left hand and instruct them to join it with a different person other than the person whose right hand they are holding. Make sure that they are not holding the hand of a person next to them. These instructions should result in a tangled mass of arms in the middle of the circle, hence a Human Knot.

The group's challenge is to untangle themselves while still hanging on to each other's hands. The players can rotate their wrists and hands for comfort but they must remain in contact with each other throughout the entire exercise. The goal is to get the group into one large complete circle or two smaller interconnected circles (much like two rings joined together.) The group should continue the challenge until one of the two goals is achieved. To eventually add a greater degree of difficulty to the exercise, challenge the group to complete it without talking.

Groups of six tend to accomplish the goal pretty quickly—usually no more than a minute or two. Larger groups can take more time, from five to 20 minutes or longer. If a group is struggling and becoming frustrated after several efforts, you can present them with a choice. They can either proceed as is or they can begin again with a second attempt by untangling and then re-tangling their arms in a different configuration. Stress that the decision must be a unanimous group decision. Rarely is a solution not possible. If however, the team cannot complete the challenge, allow them to start over and you can make the point that some issues require different approaches.

Discussion

Begin by asking your players how the exercise relates to the team. Ask them to compare what they needed to do to successfully complete the challenge to what the team will need to do during the season. You can go around and have each of your players describe an important team characteristic of the exercise as well as getting them to express how they thought and felt during the challenge. Let them lead the responses; many of them will likely relate to the Seven "C's" of Championship Team Building. If it is not mentioned by your players, suggest to them that they will find themselves in knotty situations throughout the course of the season in practices and games. Encourage them to recognize that working together as a team will help them handle and overcome the difficult situations as well as lead them to their common goal.

CHAPTER 3

COMMON GOAL
How to Create a Team on a Mission

One of your first steps in building a championship team is to discuss and determine a common goal for your season. The importance of establishing a common goal might be better understood using the Million Dollar Cross Country Road Race example which follows.

Million Dollar Cross Country Road Race

I often use this hypothetical example with teams and in my Championship Team Building Workshops to help people understand the importance of determining a common goal. Suppose I told you there was an actual city in the United States where I buried one million dollars. You were part of a select group of 100 people beginning in Tucson, Arizona who were eligible to receive the money. The catch is that only the first person to get to this city receives the money. Each person is provided with a car to drive there. The name of the city is Lockwood. What is the first thing you would do?

Since 99.9% of the population has probably never heard of Lockwood (it's my wife's hometown of barely 1,000 people), the first thing you would do is find out where it is located. You must know where you are going before you hop in your car and go speeding off trying to get there. Without knowing your destination, all of the time and energy you spend could actually bring you in the opposite direction.

After finding a map and locating Lockwood in southwest Missouri, somewhere between Springfield and Joplin, you would then begin planning your route to get there. Hopefully, you would find the interstate highways and plan the quickest, most direct route. You would likely check into the road conditions, construction, detours, toll roads, etc. Some might think you are wasting your time with all your planning and preparation, while other drivers have already gone 20 miles and are ahead. However, who's to say if they are on the right road or headed in the proper direction? The planning time you invest on the front end will pay off because you are less likely to get lost or head in the wrong direction when you go.

There is also an assumption in this scenario which cannot be overlooked. The assumption is that the million dollars has a great deal of value and significance to all those involved. In essence, the chance for the money has to be of more value and greater potential pleasure than going through the pain and monotony of driving over 20 hours. Without the possibility of a million dollars at the end of the race, few would willingly make a trip to Lockwood (unless of course, they had family there). If instead of one million dollars, I placed a dime in Lockwood and said that the first one to drive there gets it, no one would make the trip.

There must be a compelling reason and anticipated payoff considered worthy of pursuing to justify all of the time and energy that will be invested. This reason must be embraced and shared by the entire group. The team must see the potential payoff as a realistic possibility because there is no guarantee that the journey will lead them to the prize. Getting the million dollars would be nice, but you are one of 100 people vying for it so your opportunities are limited. This is the risk that all teams and individuals must face. There is a chance that if you lay it all on the line, you still might not be the first to get there.

Obviously, for the majority of you, achieving your team's goal is not going to earn you one million dollars. While most teams outside of big time collegiate athletics and the professional level do not have the chance at a million dollars, there is something that is worth much more—namely your team's pride, reputation, character and sense of satisfaction. Those intangibles are worth much more than one million dollars in intrinsic value. It is this intrinsic value and payoff which motivates most players and coaches. For example, while Michael Jordan received higher endorsement contracts with each NBA Championship he and the Bulls won, I would argue that Jordan's personal pride and competitiveness fueled his drive to be the best much more than the money.

Taking our cross country road race example a step further, not every team begins the race with the same make and model of car. For a variety of reasons, some teams will have sleek, powerful, state of the art race cars that can reach amazing speeds. Others have Volkswagen Bugs that start to shake when they go over 50 mph. Yes, every team wants to get to the final destination first, but sometimes their lack of talent makes it extremely challenging and highly doubtful.

However, keep in mind that the fastest car does not always win the race, just as the most talented team does not always win the championship. Remember that talent + teamwork = success. If your car is not properly maintained and tuned up, gets a flat tire or suffers any other type of adversity and does not handle it well, the car loses much of its effectiveness. Similarly, although you may not be blessed with the best car in the race, if you maintain it properly, keep it oiled and hitting on all cylinders, you can pass by cars with better capabilities.

The cross country road race analogy relates to many of the same factors your team must examine before beginning your journey through your season.

Where is your final destination?

What is the potential payoff if you get there?

Why do you want to go there?

Does everyone in your car want to go there?

How do you get there from where you are now?

What is the best route to get there?

What are the terrain and road conditions going to be like?

What kind of car do you have?

What kinds of cars do your opponents have?

Is your car well-maintained, tuned up and ready to roll?

What happens if your car overheats or has a flat tire?

Do you have the necessary tools to make repairs along the way?

I encourage you to use this analogy with your team to help them understand the importance of determining a challenging yet realistic goal to pursue.

GOING FOR YOUR GOAL
Leaving a Lasting Legacy

Stephen Covey has written an excellent book called *The Seven Habits of Highly Effective People*. The book provides a comprehensive examination of what it takes for people to be successful. One of Covey's major premises is that people are born with the need to leave a legacy. This means that each person wants to live a life that matters, to make their time here on Earth count and to have a sense of purpose and significance. We all are programmed with the need to make a difference in some way, shape or form so that we can leave a lasting impression on our families, friends, communities, or for a lucky few, the entire world before our time is up.

Some people seek to leave a legacy in the area of medicine by compassionately caring for patients or even discovering a cure for cancer. Others look to leave a legacy in the computer industry with the next great technological breakthrough. Still others hope to leave a legacy on their families by giving of themselves completely as they raise their children. Finally, some people strive to leave a legacy in the world of athletics by breaking records and winning championships.

Serious athletes and coaches are motivated by a need to leave a lasting legacy on the sporting world during their careers. Athletes are driven to be known as one of the best players on the team, in the city, state, country and world. Coaches strive to leave a legacy of developing successful people and creating winning programs. Collectively, teams also desire to leave legacies on their schools, conferences and divisions. Some teams are fortunate enough to leave legacies that span the ages, such as the San Francisco 49ers in the '80's and the Chicago Bulls in the '90's. It is in exploring and determining your team's desired legacy, no matter how simple or grand it might be, that you will find a powerful source of inspiration, motivation and commitment.

Covey suggests that people must "Begin with the End in Mind." This means that teams should begin their quest for success by first determining the kind of legacy they wish to leave. You can do this by fast-forwarding your team's focus to the end of the season. You and your players should think about and determine the kind of season you would like to have even before you begin your first practice.

Mission Possible

You and your players must ask yourselves, "What could we achieve if we really put our hearts and minds to it? How far could we go if everything came together by the end of the season? What kind of season would we like to have so that we look back on it with fondness and feel it was worth all the time and energy we put into it?" The answers to these questions are the first steps in developing a meaningful and motivating mission for your team. A mission gives your team something to shoot for throughout your season. It provides you with a sense of purpose and an ultimate quest, or legacy for which to strive.

> **"Are you on this team for something to do or are you on this team to do something?"**
> —Anonymous

> **"Create a significance for the group, whether it is an organization, a team, or a company. . . Each member must feel he or she is part of something important, and not just putting in time."**
> —Coach Rick Pitino, University of Louisville men's basketball

How to Establish a Challenging and Realistic Mission

In establishing a mission for your season, it is important to take an honest yet hopeful look at the team's ability and potential. Not only should you consider what the team has the ability to achieve, but also assess what the team wants to achieve. I like to present this as, "What can you achieve?" and "What do you want to achieve?" It is in balancing the "can" and the "want" that effective missions are created. Frustration and ineffectiveness occur when the "can" and "want" are incompatible. Let's take a closer look at these two important questions to consider with your team.

"What can you achieve?" In other words, this question asks, "Given your present situation considering your personnel, strength of schedule and past performances, what is within the realm of possibility for this season?"

"What do you want to achieve?" This question examines and takes into account your team's level of motivation and commitment.

One year a player on the Arizona men's basketball team thought the team should set the goal of going undefeated in the Pac-10. While it was definitely a challenging and admirable goal to shoot for, many of his teammates thought this goal was too unrealistic given that no team had ever gone undefeated during the entire history of the conference. Additionally, the team was not really committed to the goal because they viewed it as being secondary to their primary goal of winning a National Championship.

When a team's "can" and "want" are not in the same ball park, problems and frustrations are sure to result. For example, when a team has a high degree of desire but a very small degree of ability, winning the National Championship this season is probably out of their reach. Conversely, when a team has a lot of ability, but little desire, this too will lead to frustration.

Low Ability & High Desire
Some teams want to win a National Championship but given their inexperience, lack of talent, top ten schedule and their 0 and 25 record last season, the "can" aspect is a bit farfetched. You definitely want a team who has the desire to be a champion because this motivation will help your team eventually succeed in the long run. However, setting a season mission of winning the National Championship now is likely to do more harm than good.

For example, since the Pac-10 Conference is one of the nation's most difficult as evidenced by the record number of National Championships won by conference teams, a few of Arizona's teams actually set the goal of winning half of their conference games. In reality, winning half of their games and making the playoffs would constitute a "successful" season considering the current talent on the team and the strength of the conference. When the "want" outweighs the "can" you must make sure to set realistic goals for the team.

High Ability & Low Desire

A different situation is when the "can" outweighs the "want." This is perhaps one of the saddest and most frustrating situations for coaches and fans. On paper a team's height, strength, speed and overall talent should allow them to win almost any game. However, the team lacks the motivation, desire and work ethic to be successful.

I believe that some of Arizona Basketball's NCAA tournament first round losses in the early '90's were due to this lack of motivation more than anything else (I can't say for sure because I wasn't there). The teams had several future NBA draft picks but could not beat the lesser ranked teams because the underdogs wanted it more.

Sadly, there are some very talented teams that do not have the motivation to achieve. This usually is due to burnout or personal agendas coming into play. Burnout can be due to a lack of communication, a great deal of conflict or less than credible coaching. Often the fun and competitiveness are just zapped right out of the players.

Low Ability & Low Desire

If your team fits in this category, spend all of your time recruiting or sending out resumes looking for other jobs! Seriously, you probably realize that you have a building process ahead of you. As you search for more talent, begin selling your current players on the possibilities of success. The key here is to focus more on developing the habits and processes of success rather than focusing on winning outcomes when you first begin.

Fortunately, there are several examples of coaches who were able to turn around struggling programs and transform them into championship contenders including Gary Barnett and the amazing transformation of Northwestern football, Bill Snyder and Kansas State football, Lute Olson and Arizona men's basketball, Bill Fennelly and Iowa State women's basketball, and many others. This concept will be further developed in the Turning Losers into Winners section coming up. (If you do find yourself in this situation, I highly recommend you read Coach Barnett's book, *High Hopes.)*

High Ability & High Desire

Enjoy and appreciate it! You have a great match and your players will likely put in the work necessary to perform to their potential and achieve your goals. Set your sights high and get after it.

Once the Mission is Established, Focus on the Process

We have spent a lot of time talking about the importance of determining a mission for your team. Ironically, once the mission is established, championship teams actually spend more time focusing on the process of achieving it.

Using an example of climbing a mountain is the best way to understand the relationship between determining an outcome mission and focusing on the process to get there. Before they go anywhere, climbers must first decide which mountain they are going to climb. They pick this mountain often because of the inspiring, difficult yet realistic challenge it presents them. Their outcome goal is to reach the summit of the mountain.

However, once the climbers determine which mountain they want to climb, the rest of their focus shifts to what it will take to successfully make it up the mountain. They focus on the routes, equipment and strategies necessary to successfully make the climb. They spend a great deal of time planning their ascent and making sure they have the personnel, equipment and attitudes necessary to be successful.

When they actually begin climbing, their focus is on the immediate area in front of them. If they focused ahead to the summit while they were in the midst of a tricky climb, they would likely slip and injure themselves, or worse yet, fall to their death. Thus, the climbers' primary focus during their ascent is on the immediate area around them. By taking the climb one step at a time, the climbers continually bring themselves closer to their mission with each step they take.

Similarly, when players begin their season they must first decide which mission might best inspire them. Once the season starts however, they focus on the immediate drills, repetitions and workouts occurring that day. Like climbing a mountain, if you take care of the daily process of being successful, you put yourself in an ideal position to reach the top.

Breaking the Mission Down into Bite Sized, Controllable Chunks

To help your players focus on the process of success you can break your mission down into more manageable chunks. Let's break down a conference championship in basketball as an example.

The Process of Winning a Conference Championship

Outcome Goal—Win Conference Championship.
Sub-goal—win 13 of 16 conference games.

Outcome goal—Out rebound opponents by at least five.
Process goal—go to boards 90% of time, and screen out 90% of time.

Outcome goal—Shoot 48% or higher.
Process goal—get open high percentage shots, set/use effective screens. (The University of North Carolina values the process so much that they actually grade their players on the quality of the screens they set.)

Outcome goal—Limit opponent's scoring opportunities.
Process goal—having a certain number of steals, blocked shots, deflections, charges, shot pressures, denial in passing lanes.

Notice how the process goals help your players understand and focus on taking care of the important factors that will lead to their ultimate success.

> *"Our goal is not to win. It's to play together and to play hard. Then, winning takes care of itself."*
> —Coach Mike Krzyzewski, Duke University men's basketball

The Importance of Quality Practices

Not only do you need to break down your team's mission into specific goals for each competition, you also need to take it a step further and set specific goals for each practice. Each practice is a chance to improve and make positive steps on your team's journey to the top. Successful teams focus on consistently doing the "little" things that lead to their big goals.

For example, while the six-time National Champion Arizona softball team's outcome goal is to win the championship each season, their primary focus is on the process of getting there. Thus, they divide their season goal into smaller, more manageable chunks. One of their goals is to score a run an inning. This goal is further broken down into having quality at-bats, where solid contact is made. This goal traces back even further to quality time in the batting cages which produces confident and focused hitters.

Thus, achieving the mission of winning a National Championship really begins with and depends upon quality practices on a daily basis. Coach Mike Candrea emphasizes the importance of taking care of each day which, in essence, is the path to success. He focuses the players on the daily journey that leads to the outcomes that they want.

> *"What can you do TODAY that will bring us one step closer to winning a National Championship?"*
> —Sign in the dugout of the Arizona Softball team

> *today + today + today + today + today = successful mission*
> —Ken Ravizza & Tom Hanson, authors of *Heads Up Baseball*

In planning your practices, determine two or three major goals that you would like to achieve for each practice. Ask yourself, "What areas do we really need to work on to get better as a team?" Plan out your practices incorporating specific drills to address your areas of improvement. As you begin your practice, talk to your players about what you want to accomplish that day and how working hard on the drills will help you do that. Also, have each player pick a couple of specific areas they want to improve during practice and encourage them to set goals to develop those skills. Your players must learn to use each day to their advantage.

Invest in Your Success

Adapting an analogy from Colorado football coach Gary Barnett's excellent book, *High Hopes,* I have used pennies to symbolize the connection between quality days and the long term mission. Each penny symbolizes a day. Viewed separately, one day might not seem like it is worth a lot. However, when you begin to add up days into weeks, months and seasons, they begin to have much more impact and worth. Encourage your players to invest in their success. Each day a player makes a choice to use the day to his advantage, he should save a penny in a jar. Each day that he does not take advantage of, he should throw a penny in the trash can. By investing in their success on a daily basis, your players multiply their investments so that the team can gain a large payoff in the end.

Help your players recognize that they have a choice in deciding how they use their day. Each day provides them with hundreds of choices that will either help or hinder their success. For example, when the alarm clock rings at 6:00 a.m. the player has the choice to get up and run three miles to start his day, procrastinate and hit the snooze alarm, or shut the alarm off and go back to sleep for another three hours.

When he gets up, he's faced with another choice of what to eat for breakfast. He can fix a healthy breakfast for himself or have three doughnuts. Later, he can choose to go to open gym, the batting cages or a friend's house to play video games. Even if he makes the choice of going to open gym, there again he is faced with the choice of doing a tough, individual workout or fooling around and jacking up half court shots.

It is critical that your players understand their responsibility to make choices because it's their daily decisions which determine your destiny. It is these choices that either position your team to achieve your mission or keep you from reaching your potential. Your players must recognize the power of their short term choices and how they ultimately connect to your long term mission.

Using Missions and Goals
to Turn Losers into Winners

Coaches who successfully turn around losing programs use a combination of outcome missions and process goals. Typically when they are first hired, coaches talk about eventually bringing the team to a competitive level and winning conference and National Championships. However, this mission is generally expected to happen four or five years down the road. The first few seasons are spent bringing in the type of people, attitudes and standards to form the necessary and important foundation for success. Coaches focus on getting the processes in place that will give them the best chance to achieve the future outcomes they want. Occasionally, they may set some outcome missions of winning at least 50% of their games or making it to the playoffs in their second or third season, but their primary focus is on the process of being successful.

When women's basketball Coach Joan Bonvicini moved from Long Beach State, a perennial Final Four contender, to an Arizona team that had only one winning record in school history, the initial focus was more on the process goals. Rather than saying they were going to win the Pac-10 Championship in her first season, which wasn't realistic, they set a process based goal. Their mission was to begin earning respect. The players stated their mission to "Earn the respect of ourselves and others by being the hardest working, best attitude, most together, and smartest team in college basketball." This process based mission set the stage for the turnaround that was necessary.

Over the next few years the mission progressed to finishing in the top half of the conference, making the NCAA tournament, and advancing in the tournament. By putting the proper processes in place in the beginning, Coach Bonvicini and her team built a successful program in winning the NIT Championship in her fifth season and advancing in the NCAA Tournament in her sixth and seventh seasons.

Series of Possible Goals for a New or Rebuilding Program

1-2 seasons—working hard, developing effective standards and habits, win half our games.

2-3 seasons—finish in top half of conference, make the playoffs.

3-4 seasons—top three in conference, advance in playoffs and contend for championship.

4-5 seasons—compete for conference championship, finalist in state/ National Championship.

5-6 seasons—win conference championship, finalist/winner of state/National Championship.

Northwestern Football's Mission for the 1995 Rose Bowl Season

As described in *High Hopes,* Coach Gary Barnett created a series of process goals to position his team to achieve their mission for the 1995 season. These goals gave the team something specific and meaningful to strive for as they shocked the nation and advanced to the Rose Bowl.

Northwestern Football's Five Goals

1. Right Attitude and Chemistry

2. Become Known as a "Relentless" Team

3. Winning Season

4. Reach a Bowl Game

5. Rose Bowl

Adjust Your Mission If Necessary

Outcome missions like winning conference and National Championships, going undefeated at home or winning 50% of your games are definitely compelling goals. However, they are dependent on a lot of factors outside of your control. The talent of opponents, injuries, luck and a variety of other external factors impact these outcomes. Thus, you need to be somewhat flexible if circumstances change during your season.

For example, a college football team could begin the season focused on winning a National Championship. However, if their team loses the first game of the season on a fluke play in the last seconds and then loses the second game because 20 guys on the team had food poisoning, what happens to the other nine games in the season since they are most likely out of the running for the National Championship? Obviously, this situation may call for a reevaluation of the mission and to create an adjusted mission based on the team's present condition. An adjusted mission may be to position themselves for a major bowl game by playing well and winning out the rest of the season.

TOGETHER EVERYONE ACHIEVES MORE

Not only do you need to determine a mission for your season, you also need to have players who are willing to sacrifice their individual interests to get there. A common goal requires players to sacrifice some individual glory in an effort to achieve greater team success.

I remember back in the 1993-94 men's basketball season where Arizona had two future NBA first round draft picks in Damon Stoudamire and Khalid Reeves. While Damon and Khalid got most of the shots, the willingness of other players like Reggie Geary, Ray Owes, Joseph Blair and Corey Williams to sacrifice their points and play the unheralded roles helped propel the team to the Final Four. Their apparent sacrifice became an actual investment as the media exposure surrounding the Final Four brought more notoriety to them than if they would have lost in the Regional. Their willingness to sacrifice personal glory eventually helped three of the four players become NBA draft choices a few years later.

*"Good teams become great ones when the members trust each other enough to surrender the "me" for the "we."
This is the lesson that Michael and his teammates learned en route to winning three consecutive NBA Championships."*
—Coach Phil Jackson, Chicago Bulls/Los Angeles Lakers

"The one thing I believe to the fullest, is that if you think and achieve as a team, the individual accolades will take care of themselves. I'd rather have five guys with less talent who are willing to come together as a team than five guys who consider themselves stars and aren't willing to sacrifice."
—Michael Jordan, Chicago Bulls/Washington Wizards

Surrendering the "Me" for the "We"

To achieve as a team, many individual sacrifices must be made throughout the season. You must convince your players that their individual sacrifices are going to actually benefit them and their team in the long run. They may not get the playing time, or number of plays run their way in the short term, but their willingness to help the team will pay off with an even greater reward in the end. Players need to understand that these individual sacrifices are done to benefit the team.

A similar example of sacrifice and selflessness helped the Arizona Softball team win their fifth National Championship. Going into the 1997 season, Coach Candrea had a difficult situation that seemingly most coaches would love to have—an abundance of talent but a lack of positions and playing time. Coach Candrea understood that the key to the season was keeping everyone focused on a common goal.

Because of a red-shirt year, he had two All-Americans returning at catcher for the season. One of them, Lety Pineda, made the sacrifice to help the team and willingly moved to third base. This created another log jam in the infield which stacked up at second base. Two players ended up splitting time throughout the season—Michelle Churnock and Katie Swan. Katie was a stronger hitter and Michelle was better defensively, so it often ended up that one would play the field while the other would hit. Although individually it was frustrating for Michelle and Katie not to completely play the role they would have liked, collectively they formed an effective one-two punch that helped propel the team to the championship.

Problems with Professional Sports

Without a common goal, it is too easy for individual agendas to take over. Professional sports create an especially difficult environment for teams to have a common goal largely because of the differences in player salaries. Players are rewarded more on the basis of their individual accomplishments than they are on their team accomplishments. Thus, scoring averages, batting averages and other individual stats often take precedence over team successes. Each player is basically encouraged to look out for him or herself, often at the expense of the team.

"The most difficult thing for individuals to do when they're part of a team is to sacrifice. . . The Lakers made a covenant with each other to put aside selfishness so that the team can achieve it's goals, saying, 'Whatever it takes for the team to win, I'll do it.'"
—Pat Riley, Miami Heat

"Ask not what you teammates can do for you. Ask what you can do for your teammates."
—Magic Johnson, Los Angeles Lakers

Reward Team Success

In an innovative way to combat the seduction of individual stats, the Chicago Blackhawks once based many of their bonuses on team success. Instead of being based on individual statistics, honors and awards, the team's incentive clauses and bonuses were based on team statistics and successes. The management, coaches and players all believed the idea created better teamwork and success on the team. While individual honors and accolades are important, perhaps you could also create some team incentives or awards that fit with your mission.

For example, if your hockey team limits their opponent's shots on goal to a specific number you can reward them with additional scrimmage time in practice. Or if your basketball team out rebounds your opponents for three consecutive games you can end a practice early or even give them a day off. Finally, if your baseball team plays four consecutive games (or innings for some teams) of error-free defense you can host a pizza party for them. All of these incentives are based on team play and encourage your players to work together to accomplish team goals.

As a coach, be sure to emphasize and acknowledge the importance of team success over individual success. Some coaches will purposely not put their player's last names on the backs of their jerseys. They do this because they want to make sure that the players play for the team name on the front of the jersey—not just for the individual whose name is on the back of it.

Arizona Softball Coach Mike Candrea always stresses the importance of team success with his players. While he has developed numerous All-Americans and National Players of the Year, he rarely talks about individual honors and awards. Further, he does not post individual statistics. He believes that focusing on individual stats and awards emphasizes the wrong message and leads to jealousies and dissension on the team. Instead, he focuses on team accomplishments and congratulates players privately for their successes.

> *"The one thing I've decided after looking at baseball from top to bottom is that unless the whole organization is working together for one common purpose and under one common philosophy, the club isn't going to win. . . "*
> —Coach Whitey Herzog, St. Louis Cardinals

Something In Common

While many players will outwardly profess they are team players, inwardly they hope the person starting in their position plays poorly or gets injured. For championship teams, however, a common goal means that players will pull for each other. Even though the subs would love to be playing more, they still support and encourage their teammates who are playing. Instead of seeing themselves as a collection of individuals with various goals, championship players see themselves as part of a unified team working toward a common goal. They realize that everyone must be pulling in the same direction, otherwise the team will pull apart.

> *"We all must hang together, else we shall all hang separately."*
> —Benjamin Franklin

CHAPTER THREE SUMMARY
TEAM BUILDING TIPS

- Players are motivated when they have a chance to leave a meaningful legacy.

- Help your team establish an inspiring mission for the season.

- Establish a mission that is a good balance between challenging and realistic.

- Help your team focus on the process goals that will lead to your outcome goals.

- A common goal encourages players to make individual sacrifices for team success.

- Find ways to reward your team when they accomplish team goals.

- Having a common goal means that players will pull for each other.

References

Barnett, G., & Gregorian, V. (1995). *High hopes.* New York: Warner Books.

Team Building Challenge—Team Transport

Objective
The purpose of the Team Transport exercise is to demonstrate that teams need to plan and work together to achieve a common goal.

Setup
The challenge can be used with groups of three to 30 or more people. We'll use 15 people for this example but you will easily see how it can be adapted to larger or smaller numbers. You will need some towels or old carpet samples for this exercise. You will also need a moderately sized open space or a large room measuring at least 30 feet long.

Instructions
Start your group at one end of the open space and hand them three towels. The group's challenge is to transport the team from one end of the open space to the other. The catch is that the open space is like water and the group needs to use the towels like lily pads to jump across the space. The conditions are that the towels can only make a one way trip across and the team must work together to get there.

To successfully complete the challenge, your players will have to get several people on two of the towels and then pass up the third towel and lay it down in front of the team to help them advance. This process of advancing ahead towel by towel continues until the team reaches its final destination. If a person should step or fall off of a towel, the whole team needs to go back to the start and begin again.

To make the challenge a bit more interesting, you can give the team a time limit that they must complete the exercise within to be successful. The time will vary depending on the number of people, towels and the distance you want them to travel. You could secretly time the group's initial attempt and then challenge them to beat it once they completed the exercise the first time. If you are working with several teams or a very large team, you could have each of the groups compete against each other.

Discussion
Once completed, be sure to have your players discuss how the challenge relates to their team. Again, many of the Seven "C's" of Championship Team Building will be mentioned. Since we have just covered the Common Goal Chapter, have your players discuss the importance of establishing a common goal for the team. Also help them notice that it takes everyone working together on the goal in order for the whole team to advance.

CHAPTER 4

COMMITMENT

How to Get Your Players as Committed as You Are

"Individual commitment to a group effort—that is what makes a team work, a company work, a society work, a civilization work."
—Coach Vince Lombardi, Green Bay Packers

INVOLVEMENT: THE KEY TO COMMITMENT

Does it often seem like you want it more than your players do? "I wish my team was half as committed to success as I am," is a common complaint I hear from coaches. It can be extremely frustrating when the coach is one of the only people truly committed to success.

The secret to enlisting your team's commitment lies with one word—involvement. The best way to enlist your player's commitment is to involve them as much as possible in the team mission process. Why involvement? Because by involving your players you achieve two important benefits:

Benefits of Involving Your Players

1. Motivation
2. Accountability/Ownership

1. Motivation

One of the biggest benefits of involving your players in determining the team's mission is that you value and respect their goals and dreams. A large part of commitment involves getting to know each player's motives and desires. You as a coach must invest the time to listen to their hopes and dreams for the future. People are motivated by and committed to future possibilities that they believe will bring them benefits and satisfaction. Players and people in general are continually asking themselves, "What's in it for me?" When you involve your players by asking them about their dreams they begin to understand that you care about them and want them to succeed. Commitment then is something that cannot be forced upon a person, but instead, must be encouraged and appreciated. When you involve your players and learn about their aspirations, you tap into and harness the powerful motivation that is already inside of them.

Transforming "Have to" to "Want to"

Involving your players in determining their destiny is the key catalyst in changing mindsets from "have to" to "want to." Your players will begin to work hard and invest themselves in the team because they see an important connection between their present actions and their future destiny. "Have to" involves external motivation—doing something because we are told to but not always understanding and embracing the reasons why. "Want to" involves internal motivation—doing something because there is an intrinsic reason and potential payoff. By involving them, your players will take the initiative to do the things necessary to achieve the goals that they have created. It is their hope and belief in their future goals that will motivate them to work for it today.

> *"When there is hope in the future, there is power in the present."*
> —Zig Ziglar, Sales and Motivational Speaker

Without involving people in the process of determining their success, they feel as if they are coerced, manipulated, used and undervalued. Coaches can learn a lot about the importance of involvement simply by observing what is happening in the business world. A lack of morale in the work force today is primarily the result of management decisions being made that affect workers without ever consulting them. The nation's best companies and teams seek and value the insights from their workers and teammates. The best ideas generally come from the people who have an intimate knowledge of the process and the challenges they must face. The people in the trenches have the necessary experience to know what will and will not work—it is often up to the leaders to relinquish some control in an attempt to respect and serve their followers.

"Business can teach us a lot about what people can achieve when they work together. One person can only do so much. But if he gathers a company of people around him who are committed to the same goals, if he galvanizes them and inspires them and taps into their inner drive, they can perform miracles together."
—Howard Schultz, CEO of Starbucks Coffee in *Pour Your Heart Into It*

2. Accountability and Ownership

Secondly, by involving your players in determining the team's mission, they begin to feel a sense of accountability and ownership for the team. Involvement causes players to feel like their input is highly valued in determining the direction of the team. When you involve them in the process of determining your team's goals for the season, they feel a sense of accountability and ownership for their goals.

"Responsibility equals accountability equals ownership. And a sense of ownership is the most powerful weapon a team or organization can have."
—Coach Pat Summitt, University of Tennessee women's basketball

A good example to drive home this point involves rental cars—something which most coaches are all too familiar with using. Think of the times when you have had a rental car. If you are like many people, you probably have been guilty of "rental car abuse"—driving recklessly, accelerating hard and leaving your empty soda cans and potato chip bags strewn about the car. You have the tendency to abuse rental cars because you do not own them and you don't have very much invested in them. Because it is not yours, you are often tempted to treat it without care or respect.

However, contrast how you treat your rental car with how you treat a brand new car that you purchased with your own money. Odds are you are very protective of it—almost to the point of obsession. You are likely a much more careful driver, park further away from other cars and take it to the car wash on a frequent basis. Why? Because it is your car and you take pride in owning it and taking care of it.

With this analogy in mind, the million dollar question is, "Do your players view your team as a cheap rental car to be used and abused or as a brand new car that they have purchased with their own money?" Involving them in determining the team's mission creates a strong sense of ownership and registers the team title in their name.

> *"The most successful teams that I've been around*
> *were those where the players drove the machine."*
> —Coach Marty Schottenheimer, San Diego Chargers

Involving your players in determining the team mission provides them with a sense of ownership and accountability. If the team is going to be successful, it is going to be up to the players themselves. It is not only the coach's job to build a successful team but everyone involved with the program. In essence, involving your team in determining a common mission transforms the team from "Coach Smith's team" to "Our team."

> *"The team itself must be the leader of the team."*
> —Coach Phil Jackson, Los Angeles Lakers

Ironically, by giving up some control of your team and allowing your players input on determining the team's decisions and direction, you often gain a great deal more. Your players will take the responsibility of the team's success upon themselves. Instead of the coach being the only person committed to and driving the team's success, all the players now are committed and driven to success. Each player now becomes responsible and accountable for the team's goal and actively seeks to make it happen.

> *"no involvement = no commitment"*
> —Stephen Covey, author of *The Seven Habits of Highly Effective People*

THE COMMITMENT CONTINUUM

While sometimes people believe that players are either committed or they are not, the level of a player's and team's commitment might better be thought of along a continuum. There are different degrees of commitment (Long, 1995). This continuum is based on the degree to which the player understands and buys into the team goal. This model covers several levels of commitment that you may encounter on your team during any given season. Keep in mind that like team building, each player's level of commitment has the potential to fluctuate from time to time based on a variety of factors. Part of credible coaching lies in your ability to assess each player's level of commitment and to devise ways to maintain and even enhance their commitment levels. As you read the various levels of commitment, I am sure that certain players on your team will come to mind who fit with each level.

> *"To succeed as a player, as a leader, as a team, you've got
> to be committed. . . You've got to be willing to pay the price
> of success. That's a great big chunk of what teamwork is
> all about: commitment. Being committed to each other.
> Being committed to winning. Being committed to a dream.
> Commitment makes it happen."*
> —Pat Williams, Senior Executive Vice President, Orlando Magic

LEVELS OF COMMITMENT TO THE TEAM GOAL

[resistant—reluctant—existent—compliant—committed—compelled]

resistant—player has not bought into the team goal, usually because he has his own agenda. The only reason the player may be working hard is for selfish reasons.

reluctant—player is hesitant, disinterested or sometimes afraid to commit to the team goal. These are the players who usually do enough to get by when prodded, but cut corners when they think they can get away with it.

existent—team goal has little significance and the player is often participating for other reasons. These are the players who are on the team because their friends are or their parents want them to be. (This level occurs often in youth sports.)

compliant—team goal is important and the player will do what is asked to achieve the team goal. This player understands and agrees with the team goal and will abide by the team standards to achieve it. They will do what is asked of them and usually no more or no less.

committed—team goal is of high importance and the player is willing to do whatever is necessary to achieve it. These are the players who put in the extra time and energy necessary to help the team succeed.

compelled—team goal is of utmost importance and the player is totally invested in making it a reality. These are the players who feel a true sense of mission and purpose in what they are doing. They seek to and enjoy putting in extra time because they view it as an important investment in achieving the team's mission.

Other Categories of Commitment

apathetic—player has lost their love for the game and doesn't really care anymore.

obsessed—goal is the player's only focus and they have a tendency to overtrain and engage in extreme behaviors such as developing eating disorders or using drugs. Their excessive commitment gets out of hand and ends up controlling them.

How Committed are Your Players?

Take a moment and think about the current players on your team. Then categorize each player where you think they would best fit along the commitment continuum. Try to determine why you think each person is at that level of commitment. Further, start brainstorming some possible ways to enhance the commitment levels of certain players.

The "compelled" on my team are:

The "committed" on my team are:

The "compliants" on my team are:

The "existents" on my team are:

The "reluctants" on my team are:

The "resistants" on my team are:

The "apathetics" on my team are:

The "obsessed" on my team are:

Not surprisingly, championship teams have the majority of their members in the "compliant" through "compelled" categories. Further, few if any members are in the "existent" through "resistant" categories. Using this model, an important aspect of team building is to facilitate movement along the lines of the commitment continuum as well as maintaining each player's level of involvement and investment.

> *"Everyone on the team, from the head coach and top scorer all the way to the subs, assistants, and ball boys, must be committed to carrying out his or her assigned role with consummate skill, dedication, and excellence."*
> —Pat Williams, Senior Executive Vice President, Orlando Magic

*"Sports require you to commit. . . You try to play
football without having your heart in it, and you'll
end up on your butt pretty dadgum quick."*
—Coach Bobby Bowden, Florida State University football

How to Coach Your Less Than Committed Players

One of the most frequent questions I am asked by coaches is, "How do I deal with players who are not committed?" The first thing you must look at is the level at which you are coaching. If you are coaching recreational youth sports, it is tough for you to expect that all of your players will be highly committed. As many of you know, some parents sign their kids up for sports so they can get cheap baby-sitting services. You can't expect too much commitment from young children, or worse yet, force it on them when they don't want to be there.

However, the majority of you coach programs which require a strong commitment from your players. If you have some players lower than the "compliant" level, attempts should be made to call them on it and encourage their movement toward greater commitment. Have a heart to heart talk about the obstacles or challenges that are making it difficult for them to become more committed. Perhaps they are not getting enough playing time or something else has come up that is more important to them, like exploring a career or relationship interest. Help them understand both the importance of being committed to the team mission as well as your desire to see what is best for them.

Commitment ties into the legacy and mission we talked about earlier. Find out why the player started playing their sport in the first place. Ask them what they like about playing and what their future goals might be. Once you discover their motives for playing, you will learn how to bolster their commitment. Show the player the connection between the hard work they need to put in now and how it will payoff for them in the long run.

Sometimes players stay with teams despite disliking what they are doing for a variety of reasons (money, scholarships, parental pressures, peer pressures), even at the college and professional levels. Try to help them understand that they have a choice as to how they invest themselves. Also let them know that if they do not feel like they can invest themselves at a level which benefits rather than detracts from the team (at least the "compliant" level), then they are choosing to remove themselves from the team.

Watch out for non-compliant players who try to con you into thinking that they are compliant. The pseudo-compliant "Con Artists" are always grumbling and complaining behind your back to their teammates and this does one of two things. It either upsets the "compliant" team members and further alienates this person from the team. Or their complaining drags the "compliant" players down to the "reluctant" and "resistant" levels and takes their focus away from performing and on to the Con Artist. Check with your coaching staff and captains from time to time to make sure that you are not being conned by one of your players (or coaches).

Coaches and Commitment

As you look at the commitment continuum, in which category would you place yourself? Odds are that most coaches are at the "committed" level if not higher. Your commitment and love for your sport likely dates back to your days as an athlete and is probably what got you involved in coaching in the first place. Or your commitment level is high because you are a dedicated parent coaching a youth sport team and you want what is best for your children. Regardless of your reasons for being committed, it's what keeps you working all of those long hours, even though some of you are coaching for very little or even no pay.

Keep in mind, though, that you are going to be one of the most, if not the most committed person on your team. Remember that you probably played on teams where every single player did not exactly match your high commitment level but that you could still be successful as long as you had players who were at least "compliant."

Realistically, not every one of your players has to be in the "compelled" category for the team to be successful. In my experience working with National Championship teams, I would estimate that only 10% of the players would actually be described as "compelled." Out of the rest of the players, 40% would be labeled "committed" and the remaining 50% are at least "compliant." Notice, however, there are few, if any "existents" to "resistants."

Also, be careful you are not in the "obsessed" category, because that could cause some problems with your team (and for yourself sooner or later). By "obsessed," I mean that you are only focused on winning and you overlook the personal needs of your players. Obsessed coaches have the tendency to push their players too hard which often leads to burn-out. Obsessed coaches take the "Whatever It Takes" philosophy to an extreme and are prone to bending and breaking rules to win. Most players know the difference between a "committed" or "compelled" coach and one who will cross the line into obsession.

If you have rated yourself at the "existent" level or below, now is probably a good time to honestly evaluate your reasons for coaching. If you are having trouble committing to the team, it should come as no surprise if you are having commitment problems with your players. Sometimes, because of the many demands of coaching, coaches can feel overwhelmed and lose the passion for their sport. Burnout is an all too often occurrence for coaches because of their fast-paced, high pressure life-style.

If you realize that your commitment level isn't where it once was or should be, perhaps it's time to do some soul searching, delegate more to your staff or take a mini-vacation if possible to recharge your batteries so that you can get your heart back into it. For some it may be time to hang up your whistle and clipboard and find something more pleasurable and fulfilling for you.

COMMITMENT AND DISCIPLINE

A player's level of commitment is closely tied to the topic of discipline. Usually the greater the player's commitment to the team goal, the less problems you will have with discipline. Committed players understand and accept the need to abide by certain standards and rules to get to where they want to go.

Four Levels of Discipline

Investing the time to involve your players in determining the team's mission and standards also goes a long way to improve the discipline on your team. Involving your players establishes four levels of discipline: personal responsibility, team accountability, team involvement and coach involvement.

Level One—Personal Responsibility

Players will accept responsibility for and internalize the team rules and standards when they are involved in creating them. They follow the rules because they are their rules—they created them, believe in them and feel that they will help the team achieve its goals. Additionally, many times the rules they create and live by are actually more strict than the rules you would have created on your own as coach. Involving them builds on the assumption and philosophy that players naturally want to be successful and have a good feel for what needs to be done.

Level Two—Team Accountability

Secondly, involving your players in determining the team mission will help them feel a sense of accountability to their teammates. Not only is the individual accountable to herself, but she also understands that her actions affect her teammates. She owes it to the team to do the right thing.

Level Three—Team Involvement

Because the team is invested in their common goal, your players will also take responsibility for disciplining their teammates. Each of them becomes a "Disciple of Discipline." Rather than you having to be the bad guy all the time, the team will begin keeping each other in line because they care enough about the team's mission that they are willing to confront their teammates. When a person strays, your players will now begin to encourage her to get back in line because the entire team's success is at stake.

> *". . . the entire aim of our policies at Tennessee is to get our players to discipline each other . . . We have evolved a system in which . . . I don't have to do a whole lot of punishing, penalizing, or pushing them. Our upperclassmen become the disciplinarians of our team instead of me.*
> —Coach Pat Summitt, University of Tennessee women's basketball

Use your players to help decide what types of penalties should be administered when players break team rules. These penalties should be firmly established ahead of time. Typically, restricting playing time has the biggest effect on players and can serve as a good deterrent. Further, you can impose minor penalties such as carrying the team's equipment or washing uniforms if a player forgets to turn hers in on time.

Level Four—Coach Involvement

Finally, you as coach are a last line of defense in making sure your players are doing what they said they would do. You become a reminder and enforcer of the team's missions and standards. Further, your players cannot accuse you of favoritism or having a personality conflict with them because your decisions are based on the standards they created and agreed to abide by, not on your moods or whims. You confront players when they are not living up to the standards endorsed by the entire team. Thus, you not only speak as "Coach Smith," but you represent the thoughts of the whole team when you discipline your players.

CREATING A LASTING COMMITMENT

Commitment is something that must be built and maintained. Several, if not all of your players will begin the season saying that they are committed to the team goal but once the inevitable obstacles and adversity strike, their commitment soon melts away faster than an ice cube in Tucson in July. Players want to win championships until they find out they have to complete the mile run in a certain time, begin the season on the bench or they didn't realize that being on the team would take this much time away from their social life.

How many people do you know who make a New Year's Resolution on January 1 of every year and break it just a week later? (Perhaps you are even one of them.) Only a small percentage of people who make New Year's resolutions ever keep them to the month of February. Commitments are often easy to make but so much harder to keep. The strength of a person's commitment can best be measured by their actions rather than their spoken words.

*"We know what a person thinks, not by
what he tells us he thinks, but by his actions."*
—Coach Gary Barnett, University of Colorado football

Thus, part of the challenge of championship team building is not only enlisting your players commitment at the beginning of the year, but maintaining their commitment throughout the season. Their commitment must translate into consistent actions that lead to the team's common goal. Because it has to weather the storms of conflict, injuries, slumps, and a lack of playing time, each player's commitment must be strong and enduring throughout your season. In addition to involvement, another big key to developing a lasting commitment is appreciation which will be discussed in depth in Chapter Six on Complementary Roles.

Let Your Players Plan A Practice

One way to keep your players involved and committed during the season is to let them plan a practice from time to time. Former Arizona women's tennis Coach Becky Bell would assign one or two of her players the task of planning a practice periodically throughout the year. While you might be reluctant to give up this control to your players, you will likely be pleasantly surprised with what they devise. Typically, your players will plan a practice using your same drills that they like the best. While this might seem like just a fun practice for them, they will actually work harder in these drills because they enjoy doing them, plus they got to choose them.

CHAPTER FOUR SUMMARY
TEAM BUILDING TIPS

- The key to getting your players more committed is involving them and getting their input.

- To build your players' commitment, learn about what drives each individual.

- Create a sense of player investment and ownership of the team.

- Player commitment occurs at various levels and can fluctuate throughout the season.

- Teams need a combination of compliant, committed and compelled players to be successful.

- Resistant, reluctant and existent players must be confronted, understood and encouraged.

- Use your players to discipline themselves and their teammates.

- Commitment levels must be continually monitored and maintained throughout the season.

References

Long, S. (1995). *Dynamics of team building.* Colorado Springs, CO: United States Air Force Academy.

Team Building Challenge—Trust Walk

Objective
The trust walk activity communicates several important messages to your team, especially the importance of commitment and trust.

Setup
All you will need for this exercise are blindfolds for half of your team members. You can use bandanas or folded T-shirts to create the blindfolds.

Instructions
Have your players pair up with a teammate who they may not know as well or interact with as frequently. Blindfold one person from each pair while the other person will act as a guide. Instruct the guides to lead their blindfolded partner around the area for roughly five minutes. The guide should communicate often while safely leading the person through a variety of different challenges including steps, bleachers, narrow spaces and different surfaces if at all possible. The guide's major responsibility is to make sure that their blindfolded partner is kept safe during the entire process. After about five minutes, have all the pairs return to where you started.

Discussion
Remove the blindfolds and ask each of the blindfolded players to describe what it felt like during their experience. Of course, you will want them to discuss how they need to trust their teammates, especially when they were feeling unsure or afraid. Additionally, it is important for the guides to give their perspectives on the exercise. You will want them to understand the commitment, responsibility and accountability they felt toward their blindfolded teammate. Occasionally, a blindfolded person might experience a minor bump or scrape and you can use this as an opportunity to discuss what happens when a teammate is either not accountable or not trusting. Have the partners switch roles, repeat the exercise, and discuss what it was like to change roles.

CHAPTER 5

COMMITTING TO
A COMMON GOAL

How to Get Everyone
on the Same Page

While the other Five "C's" of Championship Team Building are important for building a successful team, being truly committed to a common goal is absolutely critical. I have seen a few teams succeed while being burdened with undefined roles, poor communication, disruptive conflict, a lack of cohesion and less than credible coaching, but it is extremely rare that a team will ever rise to a championship level without being committed to a common goal.

In the previous two chapters, we discussed the importance of determining a common goal with your team and creating a lasting commitment to it. The two concepts are highly interrelated. To determine a common goal for your team, you need to involve them to find out what motivates them and what they would commit themselves to doing. Additionally, your players need to be truly committed to the common goal to put in the work necessary to attain it. Since the two concepts are so important and interdependent, this chapter will provide you with several strategies to help your players commit to a common goal.

Committing to a common goal lays the groundwork for developing responsibility, accountability and an all important sense of respect and trust on your team. Let's examine a model I developed to explain how committing to a common goal eventually leads to creating a climate of trust on your team.

THE FOUNDATIONS OF TEAM TRUST

1. Dreams

Dreams are the seeds of success. All great accomplishments start as seeds of possibility, hope and inspiration. These dreams and visions of what could be are the source of individual and team motivation.

2. Involvement

As we discussed, involving your players in determining your team's direction allows you to tap into their dreams and shows your players that you value them. Involving your players sets the basis for ownership of their goals and dreams.

3. Mission

During the mission stage you combine the dreams of all your players and clarify their visions into a common goal. You should paint a vivid picture of the inspiring possibilities your team could achieve and encourage them to work hard and make it a probability. The mission provides you and your players with a sense of purpose and direction for your season. It also gives your players a compelling reason for all the hard work they will put in throughout the year. Defining a mission creates a compelling reason for your season.

4. Plan the Process

After determining your mission, the next stage is to create a detailed, step by step plan of the strategies, roles, actions and attitudes necessary to achieve your common mission. This is where you break down your outcome goal into the processes that maximize your chances of achieving it.

THE FOUNDATIONS
OF TEAM TRUST

5. Commitment

The commitment stage is when you and your players promise and publicly profess your mutual commitment to the common mission. Further, you agree to abide by the plan laid out to achieve your mission.

6. Responsibility/Accountability

When a person makes a commitment, they agree to responsibly perform certain roles and abide by the standards, attitudes and commitments valued by the team. Accountability means that each individual recognizes that her actions and attitudes affect the entire team's psyche and potential for success. Because everyone's success depends on each other, teammates hold each other accountable for their behavior.

7. Respect

When an individual is responsible and accountable to the group, respect develops because the person follows through on their commitment—they "walk their talk." Individuals earn respect when they act on their promises and commitments, proving that they can be responsible and accountable to the group.

8. Trust

Finally, only when teammates respect each other can they truly trust each other. Trust provides a sense of certainty, confidence and comfort because players know that all of their teammates are committed to the same goal. Trust is at the core of all solid relationships. When a person says that she will do something and her actions match her stated intentions, an important sense of respect and trust is built. However, if a teammate professes that she will do what it takes to win a championship, but is slacking off in the weight room and classroom, she erodes any kind of respect or trust that could be built. She is not acting responsibly by disregarding her commitment to her teammates. Her demonstrated actions belie her commitments.

"A team that operates in an atmosphere of respect and trust can accomplish unimaginable feats and reach unbelievable heights."
—Pat Williams, Senior Executive Vice President, Orlando Magic

YOUR TEAM BUILDING GAME PLAN

Based on the model previously discussed, the following steps provide you with a comprehensive way of incorporating the principles of effective team building with your team. The questions, activities and exercises allow you to tap into your players' dreams and progress through the building blocks so that you can eventually create a climate of respect and trust. While it may take some time on the front end to go through these steps with your team, the process actually saves you time, not to mention headaches in the long run.

As a coach, you know that developing an effective game plan is only part of being successful. The other part is execution. The following pages outline an effective game plan you can follow in your team building. The execution of it is up to you and your players. You need to be open, honest and committed to the process of developing an effective team. Following these steps will get you going in the right direction and will keep you on track. As always, I encourage you to adapt this team building game plan to fit your particular situation.

Interestingly, the team building process you are about to learn approaches the previously discussed Stages of Team Development (Forming/Storming/Norming/Performing) in the reverse order. You begin by having the team envision what they want to look like when they peak at the end of the season in the Performing stage. Then you consciously create and control the Norming stage by asking your team to determine the standards they will need to set and live by to reach their goals. Additionally, you discuss the Storming stage when you talk about the kinds of obstacles and distractions that could keep you from reaching your goals. By approaching all of these issues early on in the Forming stage, you effectively set the tone for your entire season.

Team Mission Meeting

The first time I used this process was with the University of Arizona men's basketball team when I began working with them in the 1993-94 season. While the team was very talented, they had suffered two consecutive years of frustrating and embarrassing NCAA Tournament First Round losses to significantly lower seeded teams. In an effort to help the team perform to its potential, we gathered the players and coaches in the locker room in mid-September, about a month before they were even allowed to have their first official on-court practice as a team. Before the balls began bouncing, we challenged the team to discuss and create the kind of season they wanted to have, the kind of season they would be proud of when it was finished several months away in April. We asked the players about their aspirations for the upcoming season.

I believe our preseason meeting did a great deal to set the tone for the rest of the season. Why? Because the players created and committed to a compelling mission before the season even started. They created a challenging, inspiring and motivating goal that they bought into before practices began. Because the mission was their own, the players set effective standards, worked hard throughout the season, and were able to reach the Performing stage and peak at the right time. While the team did not end up achieving their ultimate goal of winning a National Championship in 1994, the attitudes and processes they put in place propelled them all the way to the Final Four, and even further in subsequent years.

I use this example because I believe one of the best things you can do with your team very early in your season is to have a team mission meeting. The meeting allows your players to think about, discuss and determine the goals they would like to shoot for during the season.

While obviously you would like to add your input, it is important for you to initially sit back and listen to what they have to say. If it is difficult for you not to give any input at first, it might be a good idea to bring someone else in to facilitate the discussion. As we talked about in the previous chapters, you want to involve your players and respect their opinions. In my experience, your players' goals will be almost identical to yours the vast majority of the time.

> *"A true vision gives the team more than just a target to shoot for; it gives the team a mission, a sense of purpose to get excited about."*
> —Pat Williams, Senior Executive Vice President, Orlando Magic

End of Season Banquet Exercise

A great way to get your team thinking about the kind of season they would like to have is to use the End of the Season Banquet Exercise (Ravizza & Hanson, 1995). Have your team project ahead to their end of the season banquet. Ask them, "What would you ideally like to have said about your team? How would you like to be remembered by the fans and staff? How would you like to be remembered by your teammates and yourselves? What is it that you want to get out of this season?"

In essence, you are having your team explore the type of legacy they would like to leave. You are searching to provide a sense of purpose and meaning to your season. Ask your players, "Since you are going to be putting in over 400 hours of your time, 40 gallons of your sweat, and tying your head, heart and soul to this group, what is it all for?" You must create a compelling cause, or mission for your season.

> *"Once people know the why, they can bear almost any how."*
> —Anonymous

> *"Man will do so much for a dollar, and more for another man, but he'll die for a cause."*
> —Gary Barnett, University of Colorado football

Have your players jot down their responses to these questions and then have them discuss it with their teammates in small groups. Find out what they want to achieve and why. Then have them assess if they feel the team has the ability to achieve it. You will get some interesting responses to this one.

Have the team thoroughly discuss, challenge and debate their goals. You want to create a general consensus among the players and staff as to what is possible for the season. Ask your team, "Provided that everything comes together, what could we achieve if we really set our hearts and minds to it?" The answers you receive create your mission.

Together To-get-there: Determining Your Team's Route Together

After determining a collective destination, the next phase of team building is to specify the route for getting there. Again, involve and solicit your team's insights. If you have been successful before, your team should reiterate the key reasons why they have won. It is important to understand the reasons why a team has been successful so that they can be repeated and enhanced. Too often a team does not fully appreciate the reasons they are successful and can easily lose sight of them with the numerous distractions surrounding success. This early season meeting serves as a reminder about the important processes of being successful and the importance of respecting these principles.

Less successful and younger teams (junior high and below) typically have a foggy conception of what it takes to be successful. If this is the case for your team, you should do more directing and guiding than observing in the initial stages of the team building process. Use examples of championship teams that your team can relate to (Los Angeles Lakers, North Carolina women's soccer, Tennessee women's basketball team and the University of Arizona softball team) to help your players recognize and understand the processes of success.

I can remember sitting in the Arizona men's basketball locker room discussing the team's mission and then talking about the characteristics necessary to achieve these great heights. Corey Williams, a sophomore at the time, had spent the summer working Michael Jordan's basketball camp. Former Duke star Grant Hill, who had been part of Duke's National Championship teams in 1991 and 1992, was also on the staff. Corey picked Grant's brain about what it took to win a National Championship and shared Grant's thoughts with the team so that we could use them as a guide.

Reading the stories of other teams and understanding the processes they went through is a good way for getting a feeling of what it will take to reach your goals. I have sprinkled the thoughts and perspectives of some of the world's greatest coaches and athletes throughout the book. I strongly urge you to read their insights and ideas on their championship journeys (see the Recommended Readings section).

Developing Your Pillars of Success

Based on your team's stated mission, have them determine what it will take to get there. Ask them, "Out of the many teams vying for a conference and/or National Championship, what do you think differen-tiates the champion from all of the others hoping to get to that level?" Get your team to seriously think about and discuss the approaches and attitudes necessary to achieve your mission.

Adapting a technique called Performance Profiling (Butler & Hardy, 1993), have your team brainstorm, discuss and list the ten most impor-tant characteristics of a successful team, or as I refer to them, your "Pil-lars of Success." I call them the "Pillars of Success" because each of the factors needs to be solid and tall to support the team in reaching its lofty goals. If the Pillars are not sufficiently developed or strong enough, the team will not be able to reach the heights to which it aspires. En-courage your players to discuss and define what they mean by each of the characteristics and describe what they would look like in practices, conditioning, academics, mental training and games. (See the examples I have included from some of Arizona's teams.)

You can see by the Pillars of Success examples that certain com-monalities emerge. Things like communication, commitment, accepting roles, etc. are similar in many of the examples across teams. However, the beauty and significance of the Pillars is that you can and should customize them to the specific needs and dynamics of your team. Addi-tionally, while there tends to be a general consistency of the Pillars for a team from season to season, adjustments and changes are allowed and encouraged.

PILLARS OF SUCCESS EXAMPLES

The following pages contain examples of the actual Pillars of Success created by various teams. Along the bottom you will notice the pillars/ commitments the team believed were important for achieving their mis-sion. The bar graphs show where the team rated itself at various points throughout the season.

Team

Arizona Women's Swimming and Diving 1998

Mission/Goals	**Results**
Top Three finish at NCAA Championship	2nd Place at NCAAs
Qualify 13 or more people for NCAA Championships	12 Qualifiers
Win all dual meets	Record 7-3
Have a team Grade Point Average of 3.0 or higher	GPA 2.9

Pillars

Fun, Dedication, Respect, Confidence, Team Pride, Support, Mental Toughness, Communication, Consistent Work Ethic

Team

Arizona Men's Basketball 1994

Mission/Goals	**Results**
Win NCAA Championship	NCAA Final Four
Win Pac-10 Championship	Pac-10 Champions
Go undefeated at home in the McKale Center	14 wins, 1 loss at home

Pillars

Accepting Roles, Communication between Players, Communication with Coaches, Confidence, Hard Work, Discipline, Desire, Talent, Unselfish, Responsibility, Enthusiasm, Unity

Team

Arizona Women's Gymnastics 1996

Mission/Goals	**Results**
NCAA Super Six	7th Place at NCAAs
NCAA Nationals	Advanced to Nationals
NCAA Regionals	Advanced to Regionals
Pac-10 Champions	3rd in Conference

Pillars

Sacrifice, Respect, Positive, Keep Problems Outside Gym, Motivated, Accepting Roles, Daily Goals, Give 100%, Communication, Team Pride

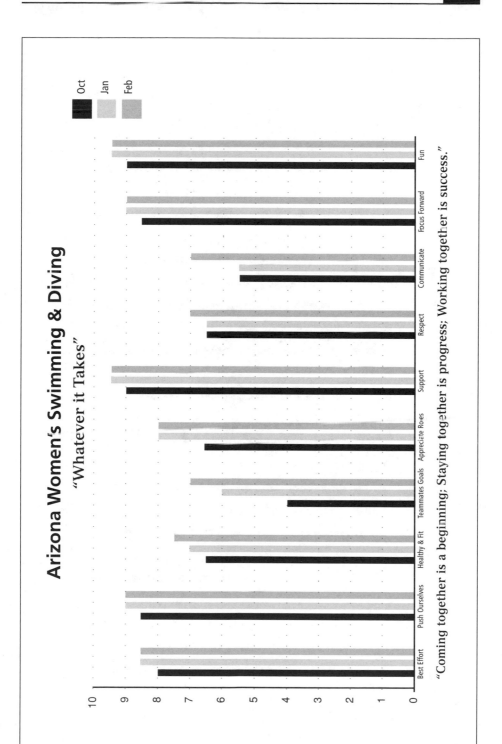

Arizona Women's Swimming & Diving
"Whatever it Takes"

"Coming together is a beginning; Staying together is progress; Working together is success."

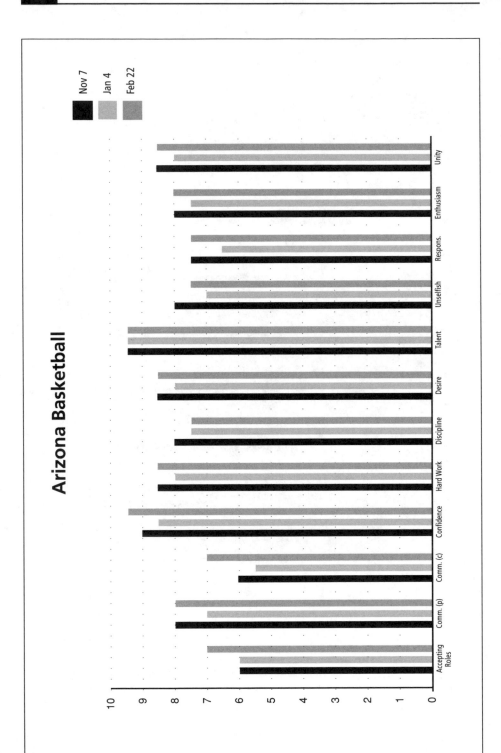

Arizona Basketball

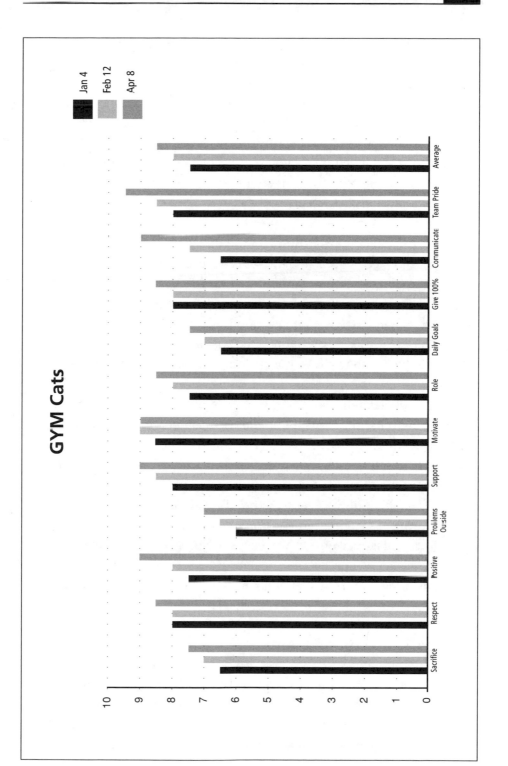

Rate Team Strengths and Areas for Improvement

Once the necessary pillars are determined, have your team assess the current height/strength of each pillar. You can do this by having the team rate themselves using a one through ten scale on each of the characteristics. Have each player individually rate the team at first so that each person takes the time to truly consider the team. Then have them reconvene in small groups as you did in determining the mission. Have them discuss their responses in small groups and have each group arrive at a rating for each characteristic. Tell them to be prepared to justify their responses as well.

List the small group's ratings on the board and then notice the consistencies and inconsistencies. Anywhere there is an inconsistency (more than two apart), give the team some time to explain and discuss their ratings. This allows the team to assess their current strengths and areas for improvement. Areas that are rated as an eight or above are obviously strengths. Ask them, "You rated this as an eight, why? What are you currently doing to make it a strength?" The team should recognize their strengths and seek to build on them.

Then look at their areas of concern (anything that is rated a six or below). Find out why they gave themselves such a low rating and have the team brainstorm potential ways to improve these areas. Discuss also any sevens, noting that they are okay, but "okay" is not going to get them where they want to go.

Use the Pillars of Success as a tool throughout your season for generating awareness, communication, assessment, ideas and solutions. It will help you discover important issues, get a feel for your team, jointly approach areas of concern and celebrate successes. It is an excellent communication tool that you can refer back to often and update on a monthly basis as your season progresses.

Creating Team Commitments

Based on your Pillars of Success and your ratings, have your players decide on the commitments they need to make to themselves and the staff to position the team for success. Make sure the commitments are as specific and action-oriented as possible. For example, instead of "Committing to do our best," make a commitment to "Be present at every weight workout and work through every set to the end." The commitments manifest the standards the team values and considers vital to achieve the mission.

By discussing your team's commitments, you consciously establish the important norms for your team's success. Instead of leaving their development to chance hoping that effective standards will eventually be established, you proactively create them with the help of your team. Together you determine the team's policies, rules and standards in alignment with your mission. You determine your team's best, most effective routes for getting to your intended destination.

When your players determine their own policies and standards, they are much more likely to understand and abide by them. They realize the significance and importance of the commitments because they see them as the path to achieving their mission.

After listing, discussing and reaching a general consensus on the necessary commitments, put them on a sheet of paper. Send the commitments list home with each player for a few days. Have your players think about the importance of these commitments to pursuing your team's mission as well as their willingness to be held accountable both personally and collectively to abide by them.

If there are any concerns with the commitments they need to be aired and discussed. If a person is not willing to abide by the commitments jointly determined by the team, the player should strongly consider finding another program. However, if the player believes in the commitments and is willing to follow them, you begin to have a team that is on the same page.

Team Commitment Contracts

We like to have a Team Commitment Contract ceremony which initiates, honors and solidifies each player's commitment to the team. The team missions are usually put on a special parchment paper and each player is asked to sign the sheet to signify her full commitment to the team. In essence, each player willingly signs the Team Commitment Contract stating her intentions to honor the mission and the standards created to achieve it. A copy of the sheet with everyone's signature on it is then made and distributed to each member. You can laminate it and have them post it in their locker or in their team notebook. The original signed commitment document is then framed (see the photo at the beginning of this chapter) and placed in a prominent spot in the locker room or wherever the team gathers frequently for practices and/or games. The commitment sheet serves as a continual reminder of the team's common goal as well as the route that will get them there.

Take a look at some of the Team Commitment Contracts listed on the following pages. Most coaches talk about having everyone on the same page. The Team Commitment Contract both actually and symbolically shows that everyone is on the same page, working toward the same goal.

> *"Winning is about having the whole team on the same page."*
> —Bill Walton, Boston Celtics

Using Slogans/Themes/Posters

To further reinforce their mission and commitments, many teams like to create a slogan that embodies their mission. We held a brainstorming session with the men's basketball team and allowed each player to come up with a saying that he thought would capture the essence of the mission. We then allowed the players to vote on their team slogan and had T-shirts made with the slogan on the back. The slogans they used were "The Best Never Rest" and "Show No Love."

Slogans will also arise within the season that can serve as a rallying cry as well. We devise a special theme each season with the Arizona Softball team prior to Regionals and the Women's College World Series. The theme serves as an effective focusing point because it succinctly captures the team's mission, approach and commitments. Themes can be used in times of adversity to refocus and remind the team of their mission. They also are a good way to mentally prepare a team before a game or practice.

You could paint the slogan on a locker room wall and have every player touch it before they head out to practice or the game. Arizona's gymnasts made posters of their team commitments and Coach Jim Gault had the team put them around the gym as a continual reminder of what

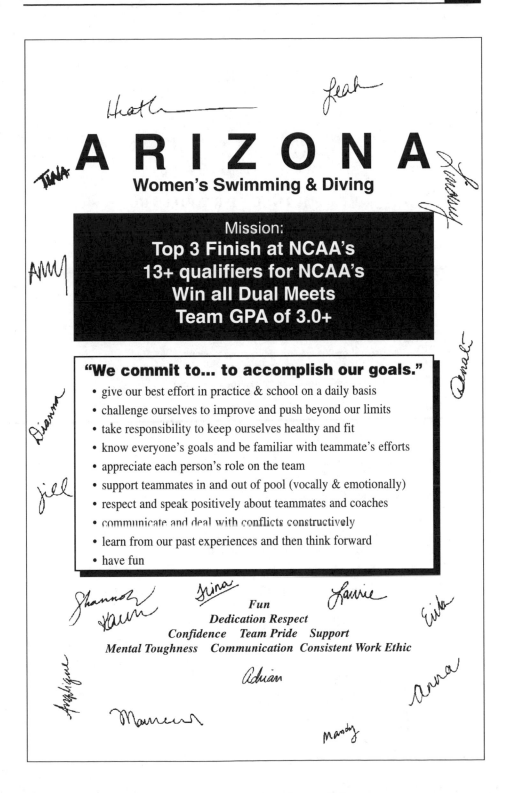

A R I Z O N A
Women's Swimming & Diving

Mission:
Top 3 Finish at NCAA's
13+ qualifiers for NCAA's
Win all Dual Meets
Team GPA of 3.0+

"We commit to... to accomplish our goals."

- give our best effort in practice & school on a daily basis
- challenge ourselves to improve and push beyond our limits
- take responsibility to keep ourselves healthy and fit
- know everyone's goals and be familiar with teammate's efforts
- appreciate each person's role on the team
- support teammates in and out of pool (vocally & emotionally)
- respect and speak positively about teammates and coaches
- communicate and deal with conflicts constructively
- learn from our past experiences and then think forward
- have fun

Fun
Dedication Respect
Confidence   Team Pride   Support
Mental Toughness   Communication   Consistent Work Ethic

1993-94
ARIZONA BASKETBALL

Mission:

NCAA Championship
NCAA Final Four
NCAA Sweet Sixteen
Pac 10 Championship
Undefeated in McKale
EFFORT IN EVERYTHING

"THE BEST NEVER REST"   "SHOW NO LOVE"

STRATEGIES FOR SUCCESS

- **Improve Communication**
  Player to Player
    Communicate with teammates early to avoid bigger problems later
      Talk to teammate outside of practice
      One on one setting
  Player to Coach
    Occasional open team forums to promote communication
    Communicate with coaches or go through team captains with concerns
    Drop by coach's office more often (once a week)

- **Improve Reponsibility and Discipline**
  Be on time to all team functions
  Monitor yourself and teammates

- **Improve Hard Work**
  Go all out - NO REGRETS
  Don't cheat yourself, teammates, staff

- **Consistent Focus in Practice and Games**
  Take responsibility to be mentally prepared for every practice and game
  Have quality practices and games from start to finish

Sign below if you are
  Totally committed to the MISSION and the Strategies for Success

ARIZONA GYMCATS

Mission:
NCAA Super Six
Pac-1O Champions

We commit to:

- *believe in ourselves and our ability to accomplish our mission*

- *accept and respect each other's differences to create unity and strength*

- *enjoy the opportunities/experiences of being a championship team*

- *bring a green light, contagious attitude into every situation*

- *give and accept support, encouragement, and challenge from each other*

- *consistently give our best effort in workouts and meets*

- *communicate openly with teammates and coaches*

- *take pride in each other's successes as if they were our own*

- *focus on quality workouts from the moment we enter the gym*

- *sacrifice our personal desires for the greater good of the team*

they needed to do to reach their goals. When a gymnast got discouraged or frustrated she simply had to look up a the posters on the walls to remind herself that her hard work was worth the effort.

ONGOING COMMUNICATION IS KEY

The process of getting your team to determine and commit to a common goal essentially centers around open and honest communication. By listening to your players goals and dreams, you tap into the powerful source of motivation inside of them. You invest the time to discuss their goals and empower them to create the standards necessary to achieve their mission. As your season progresses, it is critical to regularly revisit the viability of your mission, reevaluate your Pillars of Success and reaffirm your commitments. Ongoing communication throughout your season goes a long way to keep your team committed to their common goal.

CHAPTER FIVE SUMMARY
TEAM BUILDING TIPS

- Committing to a common goal lays the foundation for developing team responsibility, accountability, respect and trust.

- Determine a team mission early on in your season with input from your players.

- Create your own "Pillars of Success" to help your team rise to great heights.

- Have your players decide on the commitments they need to make to achieve your mission.

- Create a team commitment contract and have each of your players sign it.

- Create slogans, signs and other ways to continually remind your team of their commitments.

References
Butler, R.J., & Hardy, L. (1992). The performance profile: Theory and
    application. *The Sport Psychologist, 6*, 253-264.
Ravizza, K. & Hanson, T. (1995). *Heads up baseball.* Indianapolis, IN: Masters
    Press.

Team Building Challenge—Tire Sing Along

Objective
The Tire Sing Along presents players with a challenge where they need to strategize, commit and persevere to achieve a common goal.

Setup
Find an open area and locate an old used car/truck/tractor tire without a rim. Depending on the size of your team you may need more than one tire. Typically one car tire can hold roughly 10-12 people (more if they are gymnasts and less if they are football players). If you are using multiple tires, arrange them so they are at least 20 feet away from each other. If you do not have easy access to car tires, you can use small, stable blocks of wood.

Instructions
We'll use an example of a team with 20 people with two tires. Tell your players that they must balance all the team members on the tires and everyone must sing a complete song to successfully complete the challenge. Your players will probably divide themselves up between the tires and attempt to figure out how to get everyone up and balanced on them. Once they figure out a system, they will make their attempt to sing a song. Typically they soon discover the song they picked is too long. The majority of teams end up singing "Row, Row, Row Your Boat." If you have multiple groups, many times one group will get it first and think they are finished. Remind them that the whole team needs to be up on the tire and singing the entire song in unison to successfully complete the challenge.

Discussion
As usual, gather your players in a circle and ask them to comment on the team principles emphasized by the exercise. Ask them to share something they learned about themselves or a teammate in trying to complete it. Typically, it should take your players several attempts to accomplish the challenge so be sure to ask them about the strategies and adjustments they had to make. You can also ask them about how well they thought they handled any adversity they might have encountered.

CHAPTER 6

COMPLEMENTARY ROLES
How to Get on a Roll with Roles

"Some people believe you win with the five best players, but I found out that you win with the five who fit together best."
—Coach Red Auerbach, Boston Celtics

THE IMPORTANCE OF ROLE PLAYING

Role playing is another characteristic of a championship team. As Red Auerbach alluded to above, you are not always looking to play your best players, but the ones who play together best as a team. Most players vie for the glamour roles of leading scorer, home run hitter, running back, etc. But when your other players are not willing to play the sometimes obscure and under appreciated roles of defensive stopper, bullpen catcher and long snapper, your team is headed for trouble.

I have seen some extremely talented teams that never played to their potential because every player wanted to be the star. Most of the players were concerned with their personal stats so that the scouts would notice them. They were always looking to "get theirs" at every opportunity. No one wanted to do the "dirty work" that needed to be done to create a championship team. Championship teams have players who willingly do the tough, obscure and under appreciated jobs, and actually take pride in doing them.

"When everybody carries out his or her assigned role, a team of good, well-balanced, synchronized players can knock off a team of megatalents who are just out to pump up their stats."
—Pat Williams, Senior Executive Vice President, Orlando Magic

Arizona Basketball's MVP Who Rarely Played

The 1997 Arizona men's basketball team made an amazing run in winning the NCAA Championship. Along the way, the fourth seeded Wildcats beat three #1 seeds (Kansas, North Carolina, Kentucky) to stun the nation and win the championship. While Miles Simon was deservedly named the tournament's Most Outstanding Player and pictured on the cover of *Sports Illustrated,* the team's Most Valuable Player was ironically a seldom-used, 5'11" guard named Josh Pastner.

All season long, despite experts saying the team was too young, Josh believed the team could win the National Championship. He spent countless hours rebounding for freshmen guard Mike Bibby to help him perfect his jumper. He put in many late nights breaking down tape with the coaches to pinpoint the weaknesses of their opponents. While he played only a few minutes during the entire season, mostly at the end of lopsided games, Josh contributed to the team in so many critical ways that the players and coaches were convinced they would not have won the championship without him. Despite not playing a single second in the championship game, Josh Pastner willingly played a vital role on the team—and has a National Championship ring to prove it.

Michael Needed the Jordannaires

Even though he is the greatest basketball player of all time, it took Michael Jordan seven years to win his first championship. Jordan didn't win until the Bulls acquired the right role players and he learned to trust them instead of trying to do everything on his own.

The six-time NBA World Champion Chicago Bulls were a great example of a team that had players who played complementary roles. Obviously, Michael Jordan and Scottie Pippen were the team's primary scorers and also ran the offense. When defenses double teamed Jordan or Pippen, the Bulls relied on spot up shooter Steve Kerr to make them pay with a three pointer. Clinical sport psychology case study Dennis

Rodman played an important role of offensive and defensive rebounder as well as low-post defender. Ron Harper often matched up with the opponent's best scoring guard or small forward. Toni Kukoc came in and provided scoring off the bench. Luc Longley rebounded and did some scoring to take the pressure off of Jordan and Pippen. The Bulls were a perfect example of a team with two superstars and a contingent of highly effective role players who dominated the NBA in the 1990's.

In fact, while Jordan hit several big shots to win games throughout the Bulls six year run, including the championship series winner in 1998, it was two role players who hit the clutch, game winning shots in the 1993 and 1997 NBA Finals. Spot up shooter John Paxson played his role, found an opening and drilled a three pointer in the final seconds to give the Bulls their third title in 1993 against the Phoenix Suns. Four years later, it was sharp shooter Steve Kerr who played a similar role in nailing a top of the key jumper when Jordan was double-teamed to give the Bulls their fifth NBA Championship. By understanding and excelling in their roles, Paxson and Kerr made critical and memorable contributions to the Bulls Dynasty of the '90's.

"When we started winning championships, there was an understanding among all twelve players about what our roles were. We knew our responsibilities and we knew our capabilities. Those were the kinds of things we had to understand and accept if we were going to win championships."
—Michael Jordan, Chicago Bulls/Washington Wizards

Position/Strategy Roles

There are various roles that make up a championship team. Depending on your sport, there are obvious roles that relate to strategy and positions on the team. Point guards handle the ball, run the offense, find the open player, and hit the outside jumper or penetrate when necessary. Off guards will handle the ball somewhat but often their primary role is to shoot, drive and score.

The problem with getting individuals to play roles is that certain roles have more outside appeal than others. Who gets the most praise and all the interviews after the games? Too often it is the player who scored the most points, not the one who set the painful screens to get him open. The player who hit the game winning RBI is given all the pats on the back and not the one who laid down a perfect sacrifice bunt to move the runner over to second. Often it's the pitcher who threw the one hit shutout to win the game who is pictured on the front page of the paper and not the catcher who kept the hitters off balance with her pitch calling. Everyone wants the autograph of the running back who rushed over a hundred yards in the game but no one even recognizes the center, guards and tackles who created all the openings with their great blocks. Coach, parent, fan and media attention to the "glamour" roles are some of the biggest obstacles to getting individuals to accept and embrace less popular and noted roles. However, these roles are absolutely vital to your team's success.

Championship teams have players who not only accept these roles, but understand their significance and value to the team. These players actually take pride in playing their obscure roles. As I mentioned earlier, problems arise because the coach/parents/fans/media can sometimes make it seem that some roles are more important than others. Human nature makes it easy for people to get upset when they aren't appreciated. However, successful teams have role players who are appreciated by their teammates and coaches. They put more credibility in what their teammates and coaches think of them than what outsiders think.

"Champions separate the important from the unimportant. They know that good press, playing time or individual honors aren't as important as knowing that you and your teammates have responded to the challenge together."
—Coach Don Shaw, Stanford University women's volleyball

"Recognize the people who get less attention in the group because they're not in the glamorous positions . . . Thank them publicly for their unselfishness and do it in front of their peers."
—Coach Rick Pitino, University of Louisville men's basketball

Social Roles

Not only are there position and strategy roles on a team, but also various social roles that are played. These might include team leaders, counselors, social directors, motivators and even team clowns. Successful teams are made up of a variety of personalities who perform necessary and important functions throughout the season.

Team Leaders are the people who set the tone for the season by their words and actions. This role is critical to team success and will be discussed in greater detail at the end of this chapter.

Counselors, or "Team Moms" as they are sometimes called, are the people who take care of struggling players and are there to lend a helping hand or provide a shoulder to cry on.

Social directors are good for team cohesion because they are always planning activities and outings so that the team can socialize together.

Motivators are the enthusiastic players with positive attitudes who can get the team fired up for games with their inspirational words and quotes.

Team clowns, while sometimes a coach's biggest headache, are often the people who bring some fun and levity to difficult situations.

Each of these social roles has its place on your team. It is important for you as a coach to define and appreciate the contributions that these players make to your program.

ACCEPTING ROLES

Your goal as a coach is to have your players understand, accept and even embrace the roles they are given. When each player accepts his role and takes pride in playing it, your team has its best chance of being successful. While typically there is little challenge in getting players to accept the "glamour" roles of leading scorer, quarterback or pitcher, it's a lot tougher to get players to accept the secondary and substitute roles. How do you get your players to understand and accept their roles?

"Sometimes the player's greatest challenge is coming to grips with his role on the team."
—Scottie Pippen, Portland Trailblazers

How to Help Your Players Accept Their Roles

Getting players to accept their roles is not something that happens magically. As a coach you play a key role in helping players embrace their roles. Role acceptance depends on the model listed below.

Role Definition + Role Appreciation —> Role Acceptance = Team Success

Let's begin by tracing the model backwards. Your team's success is highly dependent on each and every player accepting their roles. In order for each player to accept the role they are given, he must feel like his role is an important one to the team's success. He must value his role and believe that he is an important contributor to the team. Players will value their role when it is appreciated by their teammates and especially by you as the coach. By communicating with your players to help them define and clarify their roles, you can also let them know how important you consider their role to be to the team's success.

Defining Roles

According to the model, the first step leading to role acceptance is helping to clearly define roles for each of the players. Role definition means that each player knows what is expected of him both on and off the court. It includes the responsibilities that they are expected to handle and fulfill such as being the closer in baseball, the defensive stopper in basketball or the center in football. The team depends on them to execute these responsibilities. Often these roles are highly specialized and limited in number.

Going back to the Chicago Bulls championship teams, Steve Kerr and John Paxson basically had to find the opening and knock down the outside jumper. Dennis Rodman and Horace Grant had two responsibilities—rebound and defend. Ron Harper just had to play defense. It's usually your superstars who have to take on additional roles. However, the majority of your "role" players just need to play their role effectively and everything else takes care of itself.

Each player should have one or two primary responsibilities that when executed successfully, propel the team toward its ultimate goal. By assigning players a role, they feel like they are contributing to the team's success in some meaningful way. Without a clearly defined role, players start to lose their commitment and are much more likely to become complacent in their work habits and disruptive to the team's chemistry.

"Molding a team begins with a clear definition of each player's role."
—Coach Jack Ramsey, Portland Trailblazers

Ways for Defining and Clarifying Roles

There are two ways to define and clarify your players' roles. These are:

1. Individual Meetings with Every Player

2. Teammates Defining Roles for Each Other

Individual Meetings to Define Roles

One way to define roles is to have an individual meeting with each player to discuss his role. It usually is best to begin the meeting by asking the player about the roles or contributions he is making presently. Find out how satisfied he is with his present role as he sees it as well as any future roles he would like to play. Either the player sees things the way you do or you need to bring in your perspective as a coach. If a player would like to play a greater role, discuss what you think it will take for him to have a chance to play his desired role. It may range from extra practice to transferring to another team. The key is to have honest and open communication between you and the player.

"I knew that the only way to win consistently was to give everybody—from the stars to the number 12 player of the bench—a vital role on the team . . . "
—Coach Phil Jackson, Los Angeles Lakers

"Identifying a player's role on a team, and having him accept it, gives him the best chance to be successful and gives our team the best chance to reach its potential."
—Coach David Odom, University of South Carolina men's basketball

Teammate Role Clarification (and Appreciation)

An excellent and effective way of clarifying and appreciating roles is to have your team define roles for each other. Have your players sit in a circle and begin with one of the players. Ask the team, "What does Jenny bring to this team? What do we need from her in order to reach the mission we have set for ourselves?" If she is a starter, the players will probably describe her current contributions and help her see her role clearly. If she is a sub, oftentimes players will talk about the need for her to push the starters to get better and to be ready in case of an injury. (See the Team Building Challenge called Strung Together at the end of this chapter).

Role Appreciation

While role definition is important, role appreciation plays an even greater part in role acceptance. It has been said that a person's greatest need in life is the need to feel appreciated. Great coaches recognize this fact and let all their players know how much they appreciate them.

I remember coaching a summer basketball camp team a few years ago. We had a great scorer, a decent ball handler and good defenders who would force the other team into some bad shots. Despite having many capable players, we could not rebound the ball. We were getting absolutely killed on the boards with second and third shots resulting in easy put-backs. Without someone effectively playing the rebounding role, I knew our team didn't have much of a chance.

I picked out a girl named Christina who had some height but was far from the tallest player out there. I told her "Most people think Billie (our leading scorer) is the most important player on our team. But what our team needs most right now is rebounding. We absolutely cannot win without rebounds and I know you are the best one to do it. If you can rebound, we can win the championship. I don't care if you score a single point the rest of the week but if you can get eight to ten rebounds a game, you will have an awesome game and help our team win."

Every chance I got within the game and during timeouts, I would call attention to and praise Christina's rebounding. No longer did she look to shoot shots that were out of her range but now she was battling for position on every possession. When the shot went up she was a beast on the boards. Christina took pride in her rebounding role and worked hard throughout the rest of the camp for every single rebound. Christina's ability to play an important and necessary role was the key to our team going on to win the highly-coveted Joan Bonvicini Hoop Camp Championship. Who are the players like Christina on your team? How can you help them take pride in their roles?

> *"It takes ten hands to make a basket."*
> —Coach John Wooden, UCLA men's basketball

> *" . . . When you're asking people to subordinate some of their individual goals for the sake of the group, you must let them know you are aware of their sacrifice. You must constantly thank them for it."*
> —Coach Rick Pitino, University of Louisville men's basketball

Helping People Take Pride in Their Roles

The way to foster role acceptance is to create a sense of pride for playing a role. Like Christina, Dennis Rodman is an example of a player who took pride in his role of rebounder. Other players may take pride in their role as the team motivator, defenseman or sweeper. You want each player to understand the contribution they make to the team and take pride in it, regardless of whether it is valued externally by the fans or media.

Six-time NCAA National Champion Arizona Softball Coach Mike Candrea is successful for many reasons but one stands out in my mind. It is his ability to truly appreciate those around him both verbally and nonverbally that sets him apart. Candrea regularly appreciates his players, assistant coaches and support staff. He even goes so far as to make sure that everyone associated with the program gets a National Championship ring including his secretary, peak performance consultant, equipment manager and even his groundskeepers.

Coach Candrea also buys several National Championship T-shirts out of his own money and hand delivers them to several athletic department staff to show his appreciation. It is his way of saying thanks and acknowledging the important contribution that each person makes to his program's success, no matter how large or small it might be. His sincere appreciation is what makes many of us take pride in our roles and has won our commitment and loyalty for life.

"That which gets rewarded gets done."
—Management Principle

Getting The Point

A simple way to acknowledge players for playing their roles is simply by pointing at them. Former North Carolina men's basketball Coach Dean Smith had his players physically point to the teammate who made the pass, or assist to set up the score. The University of Arizona softball team points to and congratulates the player who laid down the sacrifice bunt or hit the sacrifice fly to move the runner.

Pointing to a teammate is an easy yet powerful way to appreciate the important roles that must be played. While the fans and television cameras are focused on the players who score the runs, points, touchdowns and goals, you can have your players focus on and appreciate their teammates who set them up for success. They'll soon discover that success is much sweeter when it is shared.

Nails and Glue Awards

Getting players to accept roles requires appreciation. By appreciating them for playing roles, your players understand that their role is valued and ultimately important to the team reaching its common goal. While the media and fans may tend to overlook some vital roles, you can appreciate them in a more effective way through team awards.

Two such awards that I have developed are called the Nails Award and the Glue Award. One of the characteristics that we value in our players is mental toughness. The Nails Award was created to acknowledge and appreciate the mental toughness of the player(s) who is "mentally tough as nails." The award is given on a weekly basis and is voted on by the team. They are asked to vote for the player who displayed the best mental toughness during the previous week. The players are not allowed to vote for themselves. The player receiving the most votes gets the award and you can also have an honorable mention category for players receiving numerous votes.

The Glue Award focuses on team aspects and is symbolized by the "glue that binds the team together." The players vote for the teammate(s) who had the best team attitude, demonstrated by making sacrifices and/

or giving a lot of positive, verbal support and encouragement throughout the week.

You can create various awards for whatever important, yet overlooked roles exist on your team. Basketball teams can recognize the player with the most rebounds, assists, charges or screens. Softball and baseball coaches can acknowledge the player with the most sacrifice bunts or flies. Football coaches can grade blocks and reward the top offensive lineman of the week.

Simply look at your sport and find the important but sometimes obscure roles that need to be played. Let your players come up with the names for the award. Our basketball team created the "All Props Team" to acknowledge the player who best exemplified the team's standards for success. You can either determine your award based on objective stats or have your team vote for the player they felt did the best job or worked the hardest. We usually announce the award at practice, put up a sheet on the player's locker and add his name to the main award list in the lockerroom.

> *"The key to teamwork is to learn a role, accept that role,*
> *and strive to become excellent playing it."*
> —Coach Pat Riley, Miami Heat

Puzzle Pieces

Another way to communicate the importance of playing roles to your players is through the analogy of a puzzle. Get a piece of poster board and put on either your team's logo/mascot or your team's mission and goals for the season. Then cut the poster board into various pieces equal to the number of people associated with your program. Keeping Coach Candrea's success in mind, you may want to cut a few extra pieces and include your support staff members who work with your team. Hand out a piece of the puzzle to each person, giving some of the center pieces to your starters and the outside pieces to your support staff.

Have your team and support staff put the puzzle together. As they do this, help them understand that each person holds a key piece to putting the puzzle together. Without any one piece the puzzle would be incomplete. So too would your team be incomplete if one person was withholding their effort and enthusiasm. While some of your starters may have the center pieces, it takes everyone to put the entire puzzle together.

TEAM LEADERSHIP

One of the most important roles a player can play is that of team leader, or captain. Even though you as coach will be responsible for many of the leadership duties, successful teams are characterized by having at least one or more responsible, positive and constructive leaders within the team. Like credible coaches, effective team leaders must buy into the team's mission, communicate clearly, have the skills to constructively handle conflict and earn the respect and trust of their teammates.

Being a team leader is a very challenging role for many players, especially when they are younger. A good team leader must have self-control, a strong work ethic and a good attitude because they are often being watched by the rest of the team. Further, leaders must possess the tact and courage necessary to constructively confront teammates when there are problems. Leadership is a big risk for many players because they are setting themselves up for scrutiny, criticism and the chance of occasionally being unpopular with their teammates.

However, if you can cultivate effective leaders on your team the benefits far outweigh the costs. By developing effective leaders you empower your players to effectively address many issues on their own. Effective leaders make a coach's job so much easier because the team leaders also assume the responsibility of keeping the team on track. Team leaders ensure that their teammates practice with quality, are ready to play in games and abide by the commitments laid out by the team. If a person is not abiding by a team commitment, a good team leader will often successfully address the issue before you even know about it or have to deal with it.

How to Develop Effective Team Leaders

How do you develop good team leaders? Begin by looking for the natural leaders on your team, or the people who your other players tend to listen to and respect. Take them aside and have an open and honest discussion with them. Tell them that you would like them to play a key role in the success of the team this season by being an effective leader. Ask them if they would be willing to assume this important responsibility for you and the good of the team. The majority of players will consider this an honor and agree to be a leader.

Then have them talk about what they think it means to be an effective leader. Be sure to discuss what leadership means in terms of their commitment, attitude and work ethic. Also talk about their ability to communicate effectively with the team and their responsibility to monitor their teammates and to address conflicts if necessary. Finally, talk about the challenges of being a leader and that they will probably find themselves in some difficult situations.

Many coaches will place the responsibility of leadership on their upperclassmen or older members of the team. Typically this is a good idea because your veteran players have the experience of knowing how you operate and what you expect. Additionally, if you are coaching at the high school or college level, your seniors are the ones who have the extra incentive of wanting to end their careers on a high note.

"Having great senior leadership is a big key to success. It's really the seniors' team because they are the ones who the rest of the players, especially the freshmen, look up to when setting the standards. Our team will go as far as our seniors are willing to take us."
—Coach Mike Candrea, University of Arizona softball

In developing your team leaders, invest the time to communicate with them often. At the beginning of the season it is a good idea to talk with them about some of the communication and listening skills discussed in the upcoming Communication chapter. With the help of the conflict management skills described in Chapter Eight on Constructive Conflict, you also can properly equip them to handle the inevitable conflicts that will arise. Invest the time to proactively provide your team leaders with the mental and social skills necessary to effectively execute their role. It will save you and your players a lot of grief throughout the season.

As the season progresses, meet regularly with your team leaders to monitor and analyze the team's progress. Discuss any team or individual player concerns you might have and collaborate to come up with effective strategies to address them. As always, reiterate that you place a great deal of faith and respect in your team leaders and that they are responsible to honestly give their opinions as well as maintain the confidentiality of your discussions.

CHAPTER SIX SUMMARY
TEAM BUILDING TIPS

- Successful teams are comprised of players who willingly play specified roles.

- Many roles revolve around game strategy and filling certain positions on the team.

- Players also play social roles on the team including team leader, social director and team clown.

- Getting players to accept their roles is one of the toughest challenges of team building.

- Players will accept their roles when they are well defined and appreciated by the team.

- Showing appreciation for all roles helps players develop a sense of pride in playing them.

- One of the most important roles to develop on your team is that of team leader/captain.

- Being a team leader has risks and responsibilities but many more rewards.

Team Building Challenge—Strung Together

Objective
The purpose of Strung Together is to help your players understand and appreciate each other's roles. The exercise also demonstrates how the team's success depends on everyone playing their roles.

Setup
All you need for this exercise is a large ball of string or yarn.

Instructions
Have your team sit down in a large circle. Hand the ball of string to a player and have her hold one end of it. As she is holding the end of the string, have her toss the ball of string to a teammate. The original player should then talk about the things the team needs from the teammate with the ball of string in order for the team to be successful. Encourage your other players to add anything that might have been left out.

Then have the player with the ball of string hang on to part of the string as she tosses the ball to a different teammate. Again, talk about her role and the important contributions she makes to the overall success of the team. Continue tossing the ball from player to player, defining and appreciating their roles until the entire team has part of the string in their hand.

Discussion
While everyone is holding a part of the string, have your players discuss their perceptions of the exercise and what it means to the team. They will likely talk about the fact that everyone is dependent on each other in some way because of the various connections of the string. Have them talk about what it means to be connected to each other and how it relates to responsibility, accountability and trust. Get them to think about what happens if a connection is cut or a person lets go of the string.

CHAPTER 7

CLEAR COMMUNICATION

How to Keep Everyone Informed and Inspired

*"You can communicate without motivating,
but you can't motivate without communicating."*
—Coach John Thompson, Georgetown University men's basketball

Communication is another important characteristic of championship teams. The ability to communicate effectively pays dividends not only on the playing field but is also critical to developing harmony off the field. Championship teams have well-developed, open and honest lines of communication between coaches and players and among teammates. This chapter provides you and your players with tips and strategies on improving your team's ability to communicate.

Effective communication is based on sending, receiving and responding to messages. The old adage that communication is a two way street holds especially true within teams. Therefore, coaches and players should monitor their efforts to send clear and specific messages that can be easily understood. They also need to be open to receiving messages when listening to each other.

Not surprisingly, effective communication is one of the best ways to avoid and address conflict. When players don't communicate effectively, words both said and unsaid can be easily misinterpreted. Miscommunication and the misinterpretation of messages are two of the biggest causes of conflict. This means that sometimes people experience the frustrations of conflict not because of actual problems, but because of poor communication.

> *"If you can't communicate with people, you have dramatically narrowed your chances for success. Effective communication is the best problem solver there is."*
> —Coach Rick Pitino, University of Louisville men's basketball

SENDING MESSAGES

Types of Communication

Championship teams communicate effectively on many levels across a variety of situations. Coaches and athletes should recognize that different situations and surroundings require different styles of communication. The four types involving your team are: coach-player communication, player-player communication, performance communication and personal communication.

Coach-Player Communication

Coach-player communication must be a two way street. As a coach, you must be able to communicate your standards, desires, goals, feelings and expectations with your players in a clear manner. Similarly, your players must feel like they can communicate their goals and frustrations with you. One of the biggest areas that frustrates many of the athletes I talk with is that they don't know where they stand with their coaches. Taking two minutes to talk and check-in with each player on a regular basis can help them know where they stand and ease their concerns.

For example, some coaches I know make a point to say a little something to each of their players over the course of a practice. It may be anything from a "Good job" to "How are your classes going?" Players have a tendency to worry and assume the worst when they don't get much feedback from their coaches. Check-in with them from time to time to find out how they are doing and let them know what you are thinking.

Further, the best coaches I know have an open door policy with their players. Be sure that you are available and approachable so that your players will communicate with you. Northwestern Football Coach Gary Barnett has a policy that his players can interrupt any meeting he is in if they need to talk. This policy clearly shows his players that they are a priority and that he will drop what he is doing to communicate with them. When players communicate with you, make sure that you are open to them, give them your full, undivided attention and take the time to listen. Suggestions for effective listening will be given in the Active Listening section.

> *"Open, honest communication is the most important element in building trust within the program. The head coach must take the leadership role in establishing an open communication policy."*
> —Coach Pat Summitt, University of Tennessee women's basketball

> *"You can only succeed when people are communicating, not just from the top down but in complete interchange."*
> —Coach Bill Walsh, San Francisco 49ers

Player-Player Communication

Another important aspect of communication is between players. Obviously your players need to communicate on the field/court in order to be successful. You can often incorporate this aspect into your drills, insisting that your baseball team calls fly balls or that your basketball team communicates screens. On field communication is vital to your team achieving its goals. Successful teams also have a good flow of communication between players off the field. Players need to feel like they can talk with their teammates about a variety of issues.

Performance Communication

Communication during competition between coaches and teammates needs to be quick, short and specific. Often it needs to be loud, forceful and blunt. It is designed to communicate necessary game and strategy information clearly and quickly. There is no time for long explanations or to coddle someone's feelings. It is very focused on getting the job done.

Sometimes players take things personally on the field because a coach or teammate used a harsh tone to communicate strategy in the middle of the game. It is critical for athletes to understand that this short form of communication is not meant to attack anyone but to convey important information quickly.

Examples of performance communication in basketball include calling switches, asking for help on defense, getting a shot up to beat the shot clock, etc. In baseball/softball, performance communication includes calling to cut the ball, which base to throw to and calling fly balls. Without this on field communication, your team is not going to be able to perform effectively. Players should understand that performance communication is designed to deliver performance information and should avoid delivering personal information.

While communication in the heat of battle needs to be short and direct, the communication during breaks like between innings, or during dead balls can be more relaxed. Championship teams have a special ability to monitor each other during games. They can tell when their teammates are losing their focus, starting to doubt themselves or getting frustrated. Because of their common goal, teammates often have a way of saying the right thing to refocus a teammate. In essence, they know what to say to take care of each other out on the field.

Personal Communication

While performance communication is quick and to the point, personal communication should be more elaborate and sensitive to another person's feelings. Coaches and team leaders use this type of communication outside of practices and games when discussing the team. The Constructive Conflict Chapter looks at how teams can communicate off the field to control conflict and handle it in a constructive way.

Ten Tips for Sending Messages

To make your messages more effective and to minimize the chances of miscommunication, you should construct and send messages that can be easily understood by the receiver. Use the following tips when sending messages:

1. Direct

Coaches and players need to communicate directly with the person they want to receive the message. When you tell someone else to relay a message to another person, you risk them forgetting to deliver the message, distorting your message and not being able to clarify it if necessary.

2. Complete and specific

Tell the whole story. Too often we assume the other person knows what we mean and we often leave out important information. Make sure you include all the steps and details.

3. Consistent with each other

Consistency is a big key to communication. Make sure that what you want on one day is basically the same thing the next day.

4. Stated to communicate needs and feelings

Communication allows us to transmit our needs and feelings to other people. Be sure that your communication clearly states your needs and feelings.

5. Focused

Focus your communication on one topic at a time. You confuse your listeners when you jump from topic to topic.

6. Redundant

Use the triple tell technique when sending messages. a. Tell them what you are going to tell them. b. Tell them. c. Tell them what you told them.

7. At your receiver's level

Be sure you use language and terminology that can be understood by your receiver. You probably wouldn't go into the intricacies of handling a first and third situation with a Tee Leaguer playing his first game. Too often coaches are more focused on teaching topics than they are on teaching people.

8. Positive

Focus your messages on the things you want to have happen versus the things you want to avoid. How many times have you told your team "Don't foul" in the last minute of a game only to have your player commit a foul? Instead, tell them to "Play smart defense" and you will be more likely to get the performance you want.

9. Attention grabbing

Using the other person's name is more likely to grab the person's attention as well as make them more open to your message.

10. Checked for understanding

Be sure the people you send messages to clearly understand your intent. One of the best things you can do after sending a message is to ask the person, "What did you hear me say?" Hopefully, they can accurately paraphrase back your message. If they cannot, you have a great opportunity to clarify or correct what you said.

> *"It's not what you tell them—it's what they hear."*
> —Coach Red Auerbach, Boston Celtics

Nonverbal Communication

Nonverbal communication is a critical yet often overlooked aspect of communication, especially for coaches. Even though you may not utter a single word during a practice, your players can read a lot just from your body language. Dropping or shaking your head in disgust, throwing down a clipboard or giving a player a look of disbelief often communicates with more impact than any words you could use.

Invest some time with your coaching staff to discuss the kinds of nonverbal messages you send to your players. Oftentimes coaches don't even recognize the quantity or quality of nonverbal messages they send throughout the course of a practice. With the help of your coaching staff, try to become more aware of the nonverbal messages you send as well as setting some goals to improve them.

Six Guidelines for Giving Feedback

Giving feedback is an important communication skill for both coaches and players. It has been found that many of the most successful coaches give much more positive, instructional based feedback than they do negative. A study of famed basketball Coach John Wooden found that he gave a ratio of three instructional messages ("keep your knees bent, use a bounce pass, run the shuffle cut") to every one negative message ("that's a bad shot").

Keep the following guidelines in mind as you and your players give feedback to each other. The guidelines will help you create and maintain a positive team environment.

1. Positive

People respond much better to positive feedback than they do negative. As management guru Ken Blanchard recommends, "Catch people doing something right."

2. Specific

The feedback you give should be as specific as possible. For example, instead of saying "Good job" in a general way, tell the player specifically what he did well. "Good job on dribbling down to the corner to get a better angle on your entry pass into the post" is a much more specific way of giving feedback. When the player knows exactly what he did well, he is much more likely to repeat it.

3. Soon after

Give your feedback as soon after the behavior or situation as possible. If a player or teammate does something well, tell her right away instead of waiting until after practice.

4. Sincere

Be sure that your feedback is sincere. Insincere feedback will end up backfiring on you. I remember a coach who wanted to work on giving more praise to his players. While he did increase the quantity of his praise, the quality of his feedback left much to be desired. It seemed like he was saying "Good job" just to say it. His attempts to add more praise, while well-intentioned, actually hurt more than it helped. Thus, make sure your feedback is honest and sincere.

5. Frequent early, less often when learned

When players are first learning skills and strategies, use both positive and corrective feedback often as they try and improve. The early and frequent feedback will help to build their confidence when they succeed and get them back on track if they are struggling or off course. As the skills and strategies become better learned and mastered, less feedback is needed.

6. Focused on effort and results

Finally, be sure to offer feedback for both a player's effort and results. Sometimes your players will do all the right things but they will not get the desired result. However, they still need to be rewarded for the effort shown.

> *"Maintain positive reinforcement for the effort people are giving. Always let them know you are aware of it and how much you appreciate it."*
> —Coach Rick Pitino, University of Louisville men's basketball

Correcting Mistakes—The Sandwich Technique

While you need to communicate positive feedback to your players when they succeed, you also need to effectively communicate with them when they make mistakes. The sandwich technique is a great way to help players correct mistakes because it helps them focus on the correction and builds their confidence at the same time. The sandwich technique of giving corrective feedback works like this:

(+) **positive**—start by finding and saying something positive that the player has done.

(-) **correction**—build in the correction focusing on the positive thing(s) they should do.

(+) **positive**—end with a word of encouragement and hope.

For example, instead of saying, "Monica, your fielding is killing us." Try the following using the sandwich technique:

(+) Monica that was great anticipation to get to the ball,

(-) next time turn your glove to the backhand side,

(+) when you do you'll have a better chance to field the ball and then I know you can make the play.

Notice how providing feedback using the sandwich technique allows you to get the correction across while preserving and even boosting your player's confidence.

> *"Correcting mistakes is one of the most important parts*
> *of coaching . . . The majority of things a coach says to*
> *a player involves correcting him, and the manner in*
> *which you do so is vitally important . . . I feel a good way*
> *to change a negative is to add a positive to the formula."*
> —Coach Rudy Tomjanovich, Houston Rockets

Start/Stop/Continue Exercise

This technique provides you and your team with a great way to communicate about your strategies, concerns and successes. Have your team break up into three groups and discuss the following:

What things do we need to START doing to reach our goals?
What things do we need to STOP doing to reach our goals?
What things do we need to CONTINUE doing to reach our goals?

After your three groups have had time to discuss and debate these questions, bring the team back together and discuss the findings of each group. Based on the team discussion, come up with some goals and commitments you can act on in your practices and games.

LISTENING

While many people place a lot of importance on the words coaches say in their pregame speeches and post game press conferences, the most important communication skill a coach can have is the ability to listen effectively. Being a good listener is extremely important to effective coaching. It is the key to developing strong relationships with players and staff. By listening you show them you care and that you value their feelings and insights.

Effective coaches invest the time to tune into their players to hear their perspectives. Not only do they listen intently to their words, but they also are aware of the player's tone of voice and body language and understand what is not being said. Often, a player's body language and tone of voice communicates more of what is going on than the actual words used. Be sensitive to their nonverbals and let them be an important guide to how your players are thinking and feeling.

"Communicating is not just about giving great speeches. It's about allowing others to express themselves . . . The more I have listened to our players, the better I have known them and understood them. Listening has allowed me to be a better coach."
—Coach Pat Summitt, University of Tennessee women's basketball

"Over the years I've learned to listen closely to players—not just to what they say, but also to their body language and the silence between the words."
—Coach Phil Jackson, Los Angeles Lakers

Active Listening

Effective listening is an active, not passive process. It is an important skill for both players and coaches to develop. Active listening involves paraphrasing the speaker's message to check for understanding. Too often when we are listening, we spend most of our time reacting to what was said and formulating our response rather than really listening. Too many of us listen so that we can reply and fix the problem quickly. Instead, we should first listen with the intent to understand the other person.

Next time you are talking with one of your players or fellow coaches, restate what you heard them say before stating your opinion or trying to fix their problem. It might sound like an easy thing to do, but unfortunately, most of us have the habit of giving our reaction instead of seeking to understand the person. Paraphrasing what was said makes the other person feel valued because you demonstrate that you were truly listening to them.

"Seek first to understand, then to be understood."
—Stephen Covey, author of *The Seven Habits of Highly Effective People*

Active Listening Responses

Try using some of the following phrases to help get you in the habit of listening with the intent to understand, instead of automatically solving the problem or defending your position.

"What I hear you saying is . . . "

"It sounds to me like . . . "

"If I understand you correctly . . . "

"It seems like you are frustrated with . . . "

Active Listening Exercise

The following short and simple exercise can help you and your players recognize and develop the skill of active listening. Divide your team into groups of three. Designate one person as the speaker, one as the active listener and one as an observer. Have the speaker talk about a topic for three to four minutes (weekend plans, how their classes or love life is going, etc). The active listener should attempt to paraphrase the speaker's story at various points throughout the conversation. The observer should monitor the process and offer feedback to the listener following the conversation. Switch roles until all three people have played each role.

Telephone Game

This childhood telephone game is a quick, fun and enlightening way to show players how messages can be changed and altered as they pass through different people. You can divide your players up into groups of five or six and provide them with a scenario similar to the one below.

Three Costa Rican monkeys drove an '87 Dodge Aries from Las Vegas to Tuscaloosa. Their names were Huey, Dewey, and Bob. Along the way they stopped at a restaurant and ordered a hamburger, a medium pepperoni pizza and a salad. On their way they passed through Albuquerque, Dallas and New Orleans.

Show the scenario to the first person in the group and have that person understand as much of it as possible in 45 seconds. The first person then attempts to translate it verbatim to the second member of their group without looking at the scenario. Be sure the other group members are out of hearing range. Have each member continue relating the scenario down the line until the final member of the group has heard it. The final member of each group then relates what they heard. The team gets one point for each correct fact relayed and the team who finishes first gets five bonus points.

Typically, there are several differences from the original message, thus showing your players the importance of good communication and listening. Additionally, it shows the effect of what happens when players gossip on a team—the original story tends to become grossly distorted.

CHAPTER SEVEN SUMMARY
TEAM BUILDING TIPS

- Effective communication is an important aspect of team building.

- Communication between coaches and players needs to be open, honest and effective.

- Performance communication is designed to send information quickly and clearly.

- Personal communication should be more specific, elaborate and sensitive.

- Send complete, direct and specific messages at your receiver's level.

- Communication is not just what you say but also what you show non-verbally.

- Give sincere, specific, positive, process-oriented and immediate feedback often to your team.

- To effectively correct mistakes begin with a positive, insert the correction and end with a positive.

- Successful coaches believe listening is as important, if not more important than speaking.

- Listening is an important way to demonstrate that you care about your players.

Team Building Challenge—Blindfolded Shapes

Objective
The Blindfolded Shapes challenge promotes clear and specific communication and attentive listening among your players.

Setup
Find an open area or large room. You will need blindfolds (bandanas or shirts) for every member of your team and a long rope about 50 to 100 feet in length depending on the size of your team.

Instructions
Have your players extend the rope and station themselves so they are evenly spaced out along it. Once they put their blindfolds on, tell them either a letter, number or geometric shape you would like them to form as a team using the rope. The team will need to communicate and position themselves as a group to form the specified shape. Once they feel they have accurately formed the shape, have them remove their blindfolds and check on their progress. Start with easy shapes like squares and triangles and progress to more elaborate shapes like pentagons and octagons. You can also have them spell out the letters of the team mascot. To increase the difficulty and stress, impose a time limit on creating the shapes.

Discussion
Gather your group and have them focus on the communication they used to complete the exercise. They will probably discuss the importance of understanding the situation from a teammate's perspective, the need to be clear and specific, and the need to give frequent feedback.

CHAPTER 8

CONSTRUCTIVE CONFLICT
How to Keep Conflict Under Control

In addition to communicating clearly, championship teams also have the ability to keep conflict under control. They constructively use conflict to challenge and strengthen the team. Whenever a group of people with various goals, fears and beliefs is together for an extended period of time, conflict is inevitable. This is especially true when the people are competing for spots and spending a great deal of time together, weathering both the ups and downs of a typical season. It is not that championship teams never have conflict, they are just able to manage it in ways that do not interfere with the team's mission. Whatever happens, the players understand that the common goal always takes precedence over the conflict. The key is not to eliminate conflict because that is impossible; instead the key is to manage conflict effectively.

> *"Happiness is not the absence of conflict*
> *but the ability to deal with it effectively."*
> —Anonymous

> *"My job is to avoid or resolve conflict if possible,*
> *because our mission is to win basketball games . . . "*
> —Coach Chuck Daly, Detroit Pistons

Championship teams manage conflict through a variety of ways, ranging from ignoring the problem to all out confrontation and war. Part of my work with teams is to help coaches and athletes understand they have a choice in how they approach potential conflict situations.

This choice then dictates their personal success as well as influences the team's success. There is no particular ideal way to handle conflict. The best way to proceed depends on the unique factors of the particular situation. The key typically involves choosing the "best" way to handle the situation considering both short and long term consequences.

THE FIVE CONFLICT STYLES

To help teams better understand their various choices when faced with conflict, I like to use a model described by Dr. David Johnson in his book, *Reaching Out*. The model shows five different styles you can use when approaching a conflict situation. Your approach to conflict depends on your answers to two critical questions:

1. How important is it that I get what I want?

2. How important is my relationship with the other person?

Almost all conflict between people can be boiled down to these two simple questions. "How badly do I want my needs and goals met?" And, "How important is it that I have/maintain a friendly relationship with this other person?"

Let's take a look at each of the styles. Johnson uses animal analogies that accurately depict the different styles of conflict resolution. Most of the teams I work with find the animal analogies both humorous and helpful in understanding the various approaches.

Avoiding (Turtle)

Turtles seek to avoid conflict at all costs. They crawl into their shells thereby ignoring and avoiding conflict. By doing so, they hope that conflict will eventually subside or go away on its own. Turtles rate both their goals and the relationship as having low importance. Avoiding conflict situations can be a good style to use when faced with minor, insignificant issues. However, most of the time the conflict never gets resolved.

Smoothing (Teddy Bear)

Teddy Bears want to maintain a good relationship with the other person when faced with conflict and are willing to give up their personal goals to do so. They often give in to teammates in order to maintain a friendly relationship. They seek to minimize conflict by giving up what they want. These are the players who tend to get walked on and used by their more aggressive teammates. However, these are also the players who do a good job of keeping the team together during disagreements. Smoothing is a good style to use when the issue is of minor importance while the relationship is of utmost importance.

Competing (Shark)

Sharks seek to get their own way in conflict situations, often at the expense of the other person. The shark's main priority is to achieve their goals and they do not worry if they step on someone and hurt their feelings to get what they want. While you can admire the aggressiveness and tenacity of sharks, they often leave a bloody trail of offended and upset teammates in their wake. Competing is a great style to use when playing against other teams but it can have problematic consequences within your team. While the shark approach is best kept to a minimum on the team, occasionally you and your players will need to harshly confront each other when someone does something that is totally out of line.

Compromising (Fox)

Foxes are willing to give up some of their goals in order to maintain a friendly relationship. They are open to negotiating and are focused on finding a fair agreement for both parties. Foxes are often a good thing to have on a team with various wants. Because they are willing to compromise, they will eat at your favorite restaurant today if you agree to eat at their favorite restaurant tomorrow.

Collaborating (Owl)

The wise old owls are focused on helping the other person get what they want as well as meeting their needs. They take the time to find solutions that fully and mutually satisfy both people. Owls are often a rare bird on teams but certainly a prized possession.

Which Style is Best?

Remember, no one style is best but the style you choose depends on the situation. Sometimes it may be appropriate to be a shark while other situations may call for being a turtle. Additionally, while each person probably has one or two styles that they use more often than the others, they are highly likely to use all five styles at various times and with different people. You as a coach may use the owl style more often with your assistant coaches, shark with some players, fox with others and teddy bear with your spouse.

The best way to decide which style to use is to go back to the two original questions:

1. How important is it that I get what I want?

2. How important is my relationship with the other person?

As you might have guessed, the most successful coaches are focused on meeting goals *and* are sensitive to their relationships with their players. Successful businesses as well as championship teams tend to compromise and collaborate well. Instead of complaining about their individual problems, they seek common solutions to their concerns. Championship teams also use smoothing a great deal as they willingly give up their individual wants and goals for the greater good of the entire team.

Learning to be More Tolerant

Tolerance is a key component of any successful team. When I say tolerance, I mean that your players need to respect and put up with the many different personalities that make up the team. Some players will be outgoing, outspoken, zany and talkative. Other players will be more quiet, shy and solitary. It's important to understand that people have a lot of different preferences and quirks that make them unique. Teammates must appreciate each other's differences and learn to value people for who they are. Team tolerance should occur in a variety of different areas including music preferences, clothing styles, sleeping habits and anything that has little direct affect on the team reaching its goal.

However, players should not be tolerant of teammates who do things that hurt the team and its chances of achieving the team goal. There should be "zero tolerance" for gossiping about teammates, skipping practices and talking back to coaches. Deciding when to be tolerant and when to confront can be difficult. The key to making the correct decision can often be discovered by asking yourself the following question, "Are the person's decisions or actions interfering with the team's goal in any manner?" If the answer is no, then tolerance is best. If the answer is yes, then you need to figure out the best way to confront the person. The next section provides you with some suggestions for constructive confrontation.

HOW TO USE THE "DESC" FORMULA TO CONTROL CONFLICT

DESC is a simple formula that can help you and your players control conflict (Greenberg, 1990). The formula is designed to help you get your goals and needs across in an effective way while also respecting and maintaining a good relationship with the other person. It is a great way to help turtles address conflict, teddy bears assert their needs more forcefully and adds a great deal of sensitivity and tact to the blood-thirsty sharks. Providing your athletes with this formula gives them the tools necessary to navigate the turbulent waters of conflict.

D = Describe the situation.
Describe the concern/problem/behavior objectively and accurately to the other person.

You can start this by using the word "When . . . " Example—*When you are not running and working as hard as you could be during conditioning . . .*

E = Express your feelings.
Express to the other person how the situation makes you feel.

Use "I feel . . . " Example—*I feel frustrated, angry and cheated . . .*

S = Specify what you would like to happen.

Tell the other person what you would prefer.

Use the words "I would like/prefer . . . " Example—*I would like it if you would pick things up and run the way you are capable of . . .*

C = Consequences.

Tell the person the expected consequences if they do what was specified.

Use the words, "If you do . . . " Example—*If you do, I think we will be able to outlast teams at the end of games which gives us a better shot of winning the conference championship that we are working toward.*

Additionally, you may want to begin by using the person's name and demonstrate some understanding and empathy to their situation to help them be more open to your message.

Putting it all together:

> *John, I realize that finals are coming up and you have been up late studying at the library. However, when you are not running or working as hard during conditioning, I feel frustrated and angry because it seems as if you are cheating our team. I would like you to pick things up and run the way you are capable of. If you do, I think we have a much better chance of outlasting teams at the end of games which gives us a better shot of winning the conference championship that we are working toward.*

Notice that this example could be coming from you as a coach or could be said by one of your team captains or another player. DESC is designed to clearly get your message across while still being sensitive and tactful as you demonstrate respect for the other person. Of course, you and your players will not handle every situation this way, but it does provide you with a good framework to use when you want to assertively and tactfully get your message across.

The Front Door is Locked But the Back Door is Open

Another strategy to effectively handle conflict is to use someone to whom the person might be more receptive. For example, we once had a player who was involved in numerous conflicts and issues. When she was confronted by certain teammates, things often turned from bad to catastrophic. However, when a particular teammate talked with her, she was much more open to what was being said and actually would listen and become more compliant. Thus, many times we would work through the teammate who she was most open to in helping us effectively address conflict. The indirect method of resolving conflict actually worked best in this situation.

Eight Tips for Constructive Conflict
1. Begin with agreement

When you are in a conflict with someone, try to find some areas where you do agree to start off on a friendly note. Then begin to explore and discuss areas where you disagree.

2. Confront in the spirit to help

Your primary reason for confronting a person should be to show them how their actions are adversely affecting you. Confront in an effort to improve or alleviate problems.

3. Attack the problem, not the person

When you confront, be sure that you are focused on dealing with the problem, not hurling personal insults and trying to put the other person in their place.

> *"Any dispute is an opportunity to solve the underlying problem, not to inflict wounds on each other."*
> —Coach Pat Riley, Miami Heat

4. Handle individually

It is often best to handle your personal disagreements in a private setting, not in a public forum. This way you will not have the pressure of other people listening in and making the situation more complex.

5. Keep control of yourself/emotions

Sometimes it is better to wait to address conflicts. The heat of the moment and high emotions can cause people to say and do things they might regret later. Take some time to cool down and approach the situation with a level head.

6. See it from their side

When confronting someone, try to see things from their point of view first to get a better understanding of where they are coming from. You don't always have to agree with their viewpoint, but start with the effort to truly understand it.

> *"In my work as a coach, I've discovered that approaching problems from a compassionate perspective, trying to empathize with the player and look at the situation from his point of view, can have a transformative effect on the team."*
> —Coach Phil Jackson, Los Angeles Lakers

7. Don't discuss the problem with everyone else

This is often a big problem in team settings. It is often much easier to complain about a person to others than it is to confront that person. Constructively discuss the situation with the person you are in conflict with rather than infecting and dividing the rest of the team.

8. Stick to the point

Keep your discussion focused on the single issue at hand. Too many times people dredge up past irrelevant disagreements. Bringing up past problems complicates the original issue and often escalates the conflict.

Six Steps for Resolving Conflict
1. Define the problem

Be sure that you have clearly defined the problem or conflict. Conflicts within teams start superficially but are often just the symptoms of deeper problems involving a lack of respect, trust and appreciation.

2. Brainstorm possible solutions

Collectively come up with several potential solutions. Try to see the problem from a variety of viewpoints. Reserve your judgment on the ideas until several have been generated.

3. Evaluate possible solutions

Look over the possible solutions and determine the expected consequences of each.

4. Decide on a solution

Collectively try to agree on the best way to handle the conflict.

5. Implement the solution

Put the solution into action.

6. Evaluate the success of the solution

Monitor and critique the success of the agreed upon solution. If it works, you have successfully resolved your conflict. If it did not work out, you need to return to steps one, two or three.

CHAPTER EIGHT SUMMARY
TEAM BUILDING TIPS

- Conflict is a natural and inevitable aspect of being on a team.
- Successful teams approach conflict constructively which helps to keep it under control.
- People have a choice how they respond to conflict and it tends to fit within five different styles.
- No one style is the best way to handle conflict, it depends on the situation.
- Successful teams are characterized by being tolerant, cooperative and collaborative.
- The DESC formula is a good strategy for constructively approaching conflict.

- Confront to be helpful and attack the problem rather than the person involved.

- Effective problem solving is a process of brainstorming, evaluating and implementing solutions.

References
Greenberg, J.S. (1990). *Coping with stress: A practical guide*. Dubuque, IA: Wm. C. Brown Publishers.
Johnson, D.W. (1993). *Reaching out: Interpersonal effectiveness and self-actualization*. Needham Heights, MA: Allyn and Bacon.

Team Building Challenge—Conflict Skits

Objective
The objective of the Conflict Skits is to present your team with actual conflict situations and demonstrate various alternatives and consequences for handling them.

Setup
You will need to create several scenarios where players might experience conflict. I like to start with scenarios that are more general and then follow up in a second meeting with scenarios that are more team specific.

General Scenarios
Scenario One
Your friend picks you up at 9:20 for the 9:00 showing of the movie you desperately wanted to see. He/she has no legitimate excuse for being late again and does not even apologize for it. What do you do?

Scenario Two
You are at a restaurant and the grilled chicken sandwich you ordered took 45 minutes to arrive at your table. When you finally get to take a bite, it is cold and has onions on it which you specifically told the waiter you didn't want. What do you do?

Scenario Three
You generously loaned a friend some money because he said he was strapped for cash. He promised to pay it back in two weeks when he got paid but it has been

over a month now and he has never mentioned it since. Then he goes out and buys the same pair of $100 shoes you wanted but felt you couldn't afford because you didn't have enough money. What do you do?

Team Scenarios
Scenario Four
You see a teammate continually slacking off during practice when the coaches aren't looking. You also know that she told the head coach she worked hard at the optional team weight workout but in actuality she was at home watching television. What do you do?

Scenario Five
One of the players on your team got into an argument with another player and is now bad mouthing the player and only telling her side of the story to the team. Your teammates are starting to get mad and are choosing sides in the dugout right before practice will start. What do you do?

Scenario Six
A college teammate of yours is staying out late at night and frequently skipping the 8:00 a.m. class that you have together. Her grades are shaky at best and there is a big test coming up in a week. After practice she asks to borrow your notes from the past month because she has missed many of the classes. What do you do?

Instructions
Assemble your team into groups of three people. Hand out one scenario to each of the groups and have them read it. Their job is to create and act out three different approaches to the scenario. Using the Conflict Styles we discussed, have your players demonstrate how a shark, teddy bear and an owl would respond to the scenario. Between the three people in the group, have each one decide which response they will demonstrate with the help of their other group members. Give each group about ten to fifteen minutes to create and practice their skits. Then have each of the groups act out the shark, teddy bear and owl responses to their given scenario.

Discussion
After each scenario, have the observers comment on the kinds of responses given as well as the consequences for each person in the conflict. Typically, the shark responses are the funniest because the players are humorously harsh with each other. Show your players that they have a choice in how they handle conflict. Further, emphasize that each choice has an effect on whether or not they will achieve their goals as well as maintain an effective relationship with the other person.

CHAPTER 9

COHESION
How to Form a Tight Team Bond

A misguided assumption about championship teams is that all of the players get along 24 hours a day, seven days a week. Somehow people have the impression that the players skip to practice together, holding hands and singing "Kumbaya." It's just not going to happen.

Sam Smith's book, *The Jordan Rules*, provided a glimpse into the locker room of the Bulls on their initial championship runs in the early '90's. He described a team complete with jealousies, resentments and players who seldom socialized together. Even though the Bulls players might not have been the best of friends off the court back then, it appears they did have many if not all of the other characteristics of a championship team, especially a common goal, commitment and complementary roles.

Cohesion, while not absolutely mandatory for winning a championship, is strongly recommended. With a variety of different attitudes, backgrounds and preferences, players are not always going to love each other. Even though your players might not always love or even like each other, they do need to be respectful and tolerant of their teammates' differences.

Social Groups vs. Cliques
Because of the various differences that typically exist on teams, certain players will tend to hang out with teammates with whom they feel more

comfortable. Humans naturally socialize with people they like. Your players will hang out in sub-groups due to year in school, social preferences, hometowns, etc. This is normal and should be expected.

Problems arise if cliques start to form. A clique occurs when a group of players sets themselves off from the team and feels they are somehow better than certain teammates. Cliques create communication breakdowns and conflict because the different groups have competing agendas. Cliques protect their members while covertly and sometimes overtly working against their own teammates.

In his book *The Winner Within*, then New York Knicks Coach Pat Riley described a situation when he first became coach where the team was made up of various competing cliques. Riley called a team meeting and sent each of the cliques to opposite corners of the room. He told them that they couldn't be successful if they weren't willing to come together and play as a team with a common goal. By directly confronting the cliques, Riley disbanded them and got the Knicks focused on playing team basketball.

Cohesion Will Help Your Team Play for Each Other

While certainly cohesion is a goal and benefit of team building, everyone liking each other is a preferred but not necessary aspect of a championship team. However, cohesion helps your team rise to even greater levels because it gives your players another compelling reason for which to play—each other.

Most players begin to play for themselves. They work hard and persist solely because they see some personal benefits coming out of it. Other players will not only play for themselves but may be playing for their coach as well. This is often done out of respect and appreciation for the coach and not wanting to let him or her down. (How to be one of these types of coaches is covered in my book *The Seven Secrets of Successful Coaches: How to Unlock and Unleash Your Team's Full Potential*.) Finally, some players will kick it into a higher gear out of a sense of respect for their teammates. The cohesion and mutual respect discussed in this chapter will set the tone for your players to work hard and play for each other.

"There is nothing like respect on a basketball team—
toward the coach, toward one another."
—Lenny Wilkens, Toronto Raptors

"Respect is essential to building group cohesion . . .
You don't have to like each other. But you do have
to respect your colleagues' opinions and decisions,
because your personal success depends on commitment
to the overall plan and doing your part to make it work."
—Pat Summitt, University of Tennessee women's basketball

Benefits of Cohesion

1. Success

As I've indicated, cohesion is strongly related to success. Cohesion within your team enhances communication, minimizes conflict and provides you with an extra edge of motivation and commitment all because your players respect each other.

"The way we played all season—we've had something special.
We're all cohesive. We don't argue. It's great to be around our
whole program."
—Damon Stoudamire, University of Arizona men's basketball

2. Satisfaction

A cohesive team will make your season much more enjoyable for you and your players. While you are hoping to perform to your potential and possibly win a championship, reality says there are going to be several teams who will not win their last game. The experience and memories of your season will be greatly improved through the cohesion of team building.

While the championship trophies and rings are certainly nice external rewards for a season of hard work, the most vivid memories and feelings that stay with me are the special relationships formed with the athletes and coaches I have shared time, challenges, successes and tears with during the season. When it is all said and done and your players look back on their sport experience, they probably aren't going to remember all of their wins and losses or the scores of the games played. What they will remember are the relationships they formed with teammates, coaches, support staff and others surrounding their athletic career.

Having worked at the youth sports level early in my career, I believe cohesion is especially important for coaches at this level primarily for the sense of satisfaction that your children will gain. While the adult world clamors for championships, the youth levels need to remember and focus on the enjoyment aspects of sport. Unfortunately, too many youth sport coaches get blinded by their egos and end up adopting a "win at all costs" mentality. This approach causes many children to drop out of sport prematurely. The sense of satisfaction that a player gets from being on a team will help him or her stay involved in sport longer as well as build their self-esteem. If coached properly, youth sports can provide players with the skills necessary to be a successful team player in the game of life.

FACTORS INFLUENCING TEAM COHESION

There are a number of factors which affect the levels of cohesion within your team. These factors include: team size, distinctiveness, stability and shared adversity (Carron, 1993). As a coach it is important for you to consider these factors when selecting and coaching your team.

1. Team size

The number of people on your team affects your cohesion. Only a set number of players will start and get the most playing time. The others are usually relegated to a reserve or substitute role. Keeping cohesion in mind, you want to have enough players on your team to survive injuries and illnesses, but not too many that could disrupt your chemistry. Initially "compliant" players who get to play early in the season because of non-conference games can easily lapse into the "apathetic, reluctant, or resistant" mode when their playing time dwindles during the conference season.

Therefore, you want to limit the number of reserve players you keep on your team. Remember that a lack of playing time makes it easy for players to lose commitment to the team's common goal and makes it more likely for a player to become disruptive. In addition to limiting your team size to a reasonable number, be sure to clearly communicate the role you would like each of your reserves to play. Also, remember the importance of acknowledging and appreciating your reserve players contributions to the team's success.

Arizona Softball Coach Mike Candrea has purposefully kept the total number of players on his team to a smaller number to limit the number of reserves. Additionally, the reserves that he does keep are clearly informed about their important, yet likely limited role with the team before the games start.

> *"In sports, very often having too many good players is just as much a negative as having too few. Having too many players often creates jealousies and dissension, cancers that eat away at the heart of any group."*
> —Coach Rick Pitino, University of Louisville men's basketball

2. Distinctiveness

Another way to promote cohesion is to make your players feel like it is a special privilege to be a member of the team. The uniforms that your players wear for games as well as your practice gear gives them a sense of status and uniqueness which distinguishes them as members of your team.

Creating special T-shirts, pins or posters for your team is often a good way to promote the unity and uniqueness of your team. While it is only a simple T-shirt, it is amazing the kind of motivational power it has when you put your team name, mascot or slogan on it. (Just ask the fans who do not have the shirts how badly they covet them so they can be associated with your team.)

Further, you can create a special word or story that only your team knows to enhance the sense of exclusivity. Some years ago Arizona's Football coaching staff told the team a story about an ancient war. As the tale goes, a group of soldiers was to sail to an island in an attempt to take it over. The ships sailed in close to port and the soldiers stormed the island. Just as they were getting to shore, the ship's captain surprisingly set his own ships on fire and let them burn at sea. He did this to communicate to his soldiers that there was no retreating and turning back to the safety of the ship. They were either going to win the battle or die. Since retreat was no longer an option, the soldiers fought even harder and won the battle and the island. After the story, the team was given shirts with the slogan "Burn The Boats" printed on the back to remember the moral of the story as they began their season.

In a similar example, one year we created a safari theme for the Arizona Softball team as they headed into Regionals and the Women's College World Series. To add a sense of mystery and exclusivity to the theme, I researched three Swahili words (ushindi, kujiamini and timu oyee) which related to our mission. We shared the words with our players on the condition that they were sworn to secrecy about their meaning. We had T-shirts printed with the Swahili words on the back and used them to motivate and focus the team throughout the series. The secret words gave the team a special sense of distinctiveness. (Sorry, I too am sworn to secrecy about the actual meanings of the words.)

3. Stability

Another way to foster cohesion is to have minimal turnover of your players and staff. It takes a while to truly get to know someone and trust them. By spending an extended period of time with a person you tend to know what to expect from them and a certain sense of confidence and consistency is developed. However, when players are continually moving from team to team it is much more difficult to build cohesion because they aren't around long enough to know more than the names of their teammates.

Stability is a tough factor for many teams because of age restrictions, graduation, transfers, trades, free agency and coaches looking for better jobs. Do your best within these parameters to build a sense of stability among the members of your team. Treat your players well so that they will want to stay with your team. Also, make sure you appreciate your assistants and support staff and do what you can to make it easier for them to stay around and contribute to your program.

Additionally, coaches should use caution when bringing a new player or coach on to the team in the middle of the season. Sometimes injuries, transfers and other situations necessitate adding players during the middle of the year; but be careful. It can be difficult to parachute a new person into your team because you have already shared many experiences during the season of which this person has no knowledge or understanding. Further, if the new person is competing for playing time it could disrupt the chemistry you have built up to this point. The key is to be sensitive to how the new person could affect your team and talk with your staff and players about how best to make the situation work for everyone.

4. Shared adversity

Admittedly for me, one of the toughest things about my job is saying "good bye" to the seniors with whom I have worked during their college careers. We often share a tight bond largely because we have been through so much together—injuries, slumps, close losses, conflicts as well as celebrating successes. Going through tough times together is definitely a bonding experience for people.

Ask any war veteran who they feel close to and it is almost always the people in their military unit. A strong bond develops because they had to trust each other with their lives, spending many difficult days in harrowing conditions. For soldiers to survive, they had to work together as a team. Going through adversity together has a way of creating a unique and lasting bond between people.

While certainly not like the life-threatening dangers of war, adversity still abounds in the sporting world. However, it's not how much adversity a team faces during a season, but more importantly, how they respond to it. You can tell a lot about a person and a team by how they choose to handle adversity. Unfortunately, too many players blame their teammates when things go bad in an effort to protect themselves. Adversity has lead many teams to splinter, crack and disintegrate.

Because a team's reaction to adversity is so important, we will sometimes practice their response to it so that the players can remain calm, make the necessary adjustments and stay focused. Here again is where you can work through your team leaders or captains to ensure that they have the proper communication skills to weather the storm, refocus the team and get them back on track. Team leaders often take advantage of breaks in the action and time outs to make sure that the team is sticking together through adversity.

Championship teams come together during adversity. They use the adversity of disrespectful comments made by opponents, criticism by fans or sportswriters and receiving low or no rankings in the polls to motivate themselves. Further, there is nothing potentially better to bring a team together than playing an away game against a tough opponent with a hostile crowd. Adversity sets the stage for adopting an "Us Against the World" type mindset which solidifies your team's unity and strengthens your player's resolve to achieve their mission. Taking on the adversity as a team proves there is strength in numbers.

"I'm tremendously proud of this group of guys. These are guys who have been on a mission all year long. They worked hard, they competed hard. Sometimes with adversity, it kind of brings people together, and it's been an enjoyment for me to watch."
—Coach Lute Olson, University of Arizona men's basketball

TWELVE STRATEGIES FOR BUILDING TEAM COHESION

The following suggestions list a variety of ways to build a sense of fun and family with your team. As you read each one, think about how and when you might be able to use or adapt the suggestion with your team.

1. Team Activities

Team activities are a way to help your team get to know each other during the Forming stage as well as bond as you progress toward the Performing stage. Many teams that I have worked with will have team dinners, go on a team hike, go to the movies together or play frisbee football. The idea is to do something fun away from your sport. University of Tennessee women's basketball Coach Pat Summitt likes to host pot luck dinners for team building where each player is responsible for bringing a different dish. The underlying message is that if everyone takes responsibility to contribute something, the whole team benefits.

2. Preseason Retreat

Preseason retreats or training camps are often good ways to help your team bond for the upcoming season. Many football teams travel to other towns to minimize distractions and help their players bond. Of course this option depends on your budget, but you could still get away to a park during an afternoon to spend some quality time with your team.

3. Team Scavenger Hunt

In an effort to help players get to know each other better, you can create a campus scavenger hunt. Break the team into groups of five and give them a camera and a list of things they need to do or find. The team then figures out how to accomplish the mission and end up learning a lot about the campus and themselves.

Sample Scavenger Hunt

- have your picture taken with an Associate Athletic Director and get their business card

- list the three services available at the Campus Health building

- take a creative picture of your group somewhere on campus

- get the University president's signature or stamped signature from his/her secretary

- find out how you can get an internship from the Career Placement Center

- take a picture with a professor from the English department

- count the number of stairs leading to Union

- write down the names and artists of five pictures in the art museum

- meet a coach and an athlete and find out their team and personal goals for the season

- get a menu from one of the restaurants located in the Student Center

- check-out a book from the library that would be good for our team

4. People Bingo

Use this activity to help your players get to know each other and break the ice at some of the first team meetings. Sometime before the meeting have your players list something few people know about them. Arrange these little known player facts on a grid much like a bingo card. Then when your players get together hand them all a bingo card. Tell them that they must go around and individually talk with their teammates to find out more about them. They should then put the initials of the person associated with each personal fact on the grid until they have so many initials in a row or have filled their card.

5. Support Squad

The Support Squad provides your team with a variety of benefits including setting goals for quality practices, establishing accountability and helping your players get to know each other better. At the beginning of the week, pair up your players with one another. Have the pairs discuss and write down their goals for the upcoming week. (See my mental training workbook *The Mental Makings of Champions* for more information on goal setting guidelines.) Also have them discuss any obstacles or difficulties they could face in achieving their goals. They should then plan some ways to overcome these obstacles as well as how their partner might assist them.

The partners then serve as a reminder and supporter of their goals. Not only is each player focused on achieving a goal for the week, but they are also held accountable by a teammate who is there to support and challenge them. At the end of the week, have the partners evaluate each other's progress. Change partners for each subsequent week throughout the season.

Your players will eventually be paired with a majority if not all of their teammates at some time during the season. They will have a week to get to know each player as well as the typical challenges that they may face. More importantly, they will be able to assist their teammate in refocusing them should these obstacles arise throughout the season, especially in competition.

People Bingo Card

Which Player. . .

has two Samoyd dogs	had a great trip to Alaska this summer	was born in a state with one of the largest prisons	can blow bubbles off their tongue
plays the trumpet, baritone and saxophone	knows Chase Hampton from the Mickey Mouse Club	favorite color is light pink	volunteers to work with animal defense
can make their stomach talk	can make a sound like a car alarm	was born in Normal, IL but may not be too normal	enjoyed Sweden because of the discos
knows American sign language	plays the drums	has a dog named Lexus	was born in Rhode Island

Directions

Find out which teammate corresponds with each of the strange but true facts on your Bingo Card. Put the initials of the person in the corresponding box.

SUPPORT SQUAD

Date:

Name   Name

Challenge me to . . .	

Support me if I struggle with. . .	

If I get frustrated, remind me to . . .	

6. Secret Psych Pals

Arizona's women's swim team creates Secret Psych Pals. Much like picking names of relatives when buying holiday gifts, each swimmer draws a name and becomes the person's Secret Psych Pal for the upcoming meet. The swimmers secretly do special things for their pals like writing them notes, sticking candy in their locker or any other well-meaning deeds. They then reveal who their secret psych pals are before the meet.

7. Appreciation Notes

Another way to build appreciation into your team is through Appreciation Notes. Provide your team with strips of paper to write small notes to their teammates. I usually invite them to write one to their support squad partner acknowledging one of their successes for the week. You can also make them available on a bulletin board so that they can be written whenever someone gets the impulse. We then post the notes on the team bulletin board as a consistent reminder of success and inspiration.

*"Kind words are short and easy to speak,
but their echoes are truly endless."*
—Mother Teresa

8. Switch Positions

In an effort to appreciate each other's roles, have some fun and add some spice to practice, Arizona Softball Coach Mike Candrea has a scrimmage where he puts his players into positions that they do not normally play. Infielders switch with the outfielders and catchers become pitchers. The team enjoys watching their teammates struggle with their new roles while they learn to appreciate the important contributions that everyone makes to the team's success.

9. I Got Your Back

Hand each of your players a sheet of paper. Instruct them to write their name on the paper followed by the word "Strengths." The players should then tape the paper to their backs. Then have the players go around and write in the strengths they see in their teammates. When they are finished, have them read what their teammates wrote about them.

10. Confidence Circles

A variation of listing each player's strengths on her back is what I call Confidence Circles. If you have a team of around 15 or less you can get the group into one large circle. If your team is 20 members or larger you might want to break them into smaller circles of 10 to 15 people. Again, have each player get a sheet of paper and write on the top of it their name followed by the word "Strengths." Have each player then pass the sheet to their teammate on the right. The teammate then writes down the player's strengths. After roughly a minute or so, have the players pass the sheet to the right again until the player's original sheet eventually returns to her.

11. Thank You Notes

An especially appropriate team building exercise around Thanksgiving time, Thank You Notes allow your players to appreciate people they are close to. All you need are some pens and stationery. Ask each player to think of a person who has made a tremendous impact on their life. Most players pick a parent, sibling, former coach or friend, but it can be almost anyone. Have your players write a letter of appreciation to that person thanking them for their inspiration, guidance and support. After each person has finished their letter, invite your players to share who they picked and to either read the letter aloud or summarize what it said. Encourage your players to send or hand deliver the note to the person once they get home.

You can also take this idea a step further and use it to motivate your team before a big game. In 1990, the #9 ranked University of Colorado football team played a big game in Lincoln against the #3 ranked Cornhuskers of the University of Nebraska. The game was an important one in the race for the Big Eight Conference Championship as well as the National Championship.

In one of the final practices before the game, Coach Bill McCartney got his team together. He told each of the players to think about a person who really meant a lot to them in their lives; someone whom the player loved deeply. He encouraged the players to call or talk to that person and ask them to watch the game against Nebraska. He also asked the players to tell the people they loved that they were going to dedicate each and every play of the Nebraska game to them.

Colorado played some of its most inspired football of the season and came out and beat an excellent Nebraska team 27-12 on the Cornhuskers rainy and cold home turf. In essence, Coach McCartney's suggestion to his players created another compelling reason for which to play, as a tribute to a loved one. The win played an important part in the Buffaloes winning the Big Eight Conference Championship as well as setting the stage for their Orange Bowl win over Notre Dame and the 1990 National Championship.

I must caution you that this idea should be reserved for a special occasion and should not be repeated with the same group. Further, because of the aggressive nature of the sport and the importance of brute strength, this idea works well in football because most players tend to play better when they are highly energized. However, this idea can backfire when used with sports which emphasize more fine, precise movements like gymnastics. Finally, this idea often works better when your team is an underdog or you are facing your archrival. As always, rely on your coaching intuition with all of these suggestions and use what you think will work for your team.

12. Family Picture Album

This idea comes from Pat Summitt's sport psychologist, Dr. Nina Elliott, as described in Summitt's excellent book, *Reach for the Summit*. Have your players bring in pictures of their family and very close friends to show to their teammates. Allow each player a few minutes to talk about their family members and friends and their relationships with them. The exercise can be an emotional one because many players disclose how much certain people mean to them. This kind of open sharing can do a lot to bring a team together.

(Author's note: If you have any other team building ideas that have worked especially well for you, please call or send them to me and I will be happy to credit you with them in future editions of this book. My contact information is available at the front and back of this book.)

CHAPTER NINE SUMMARY
TEAM BUILDING TIPS

- Cohesion is not mandatory but highly beneficial for effective teams.

- Cohesion contributes to your team's success and sense of satisfaction.

- It is normal and natural if not all of your players like each other.

- Players at least need to be able to respect each other as teammates.

- Cohesion is influenced by your team's size so keep your numbers manageable.

- Use stories and T-shirts to create a sense of uniqueness within your team.

- Minimize the amount of player and staff turnover to enhance cohesion.

- Use adversity to help you grow stronger as a team.

- Plan occasional social activities for your team outside of practices and games.

- Create opportunities for your players to praise and appreciate each other to promote team bonding.

References

Carron, B.V., (1993). The sport team as an effective group. In J.M. Williams (Ed.), *Applied sport psychology: Personal growth to peak performance*. Palo Alto, CA: Mayfield.

Smith, S. (1993). *The Jordan rules*. New York: Pocket Books.

Riley, P. (1993). *The winner within*. New York: Putnam.

Team Building Challenge—Balloon Train

Objective
Balloon train shows your players the importance of being a cohesive team.

Setup
You will need to get twice as many large sized balloons as you have team members. You will also need to set up a short slalom course using four to six cones or T-shirts. Place the cones on a zig-zag slalom course roughly 5-10 yards away from each other.

Instructions
Tell each of your team members to blow up a balloon. Leave the extra balloons deflated for now. Have your team get into a single-file, straight line facing the slalom course. Tell them to place their balloon between their navel and the teammate who is in front of them. Have your players get close together so that all of the balloons are suspended and supported between the stomach of one teammate and the back of another.

The team's challenge is to walk as a unit through the slalom course without dropping or popping any of the balloons. If a balloon should pop or drop, the entire team needs to go back to the beginning and start again. The extra balloons at the start are to replace the ones that pop. You can increase the degree of difficulty for the exercise by having them complete it in a certain time or having a limited number of balloons available to replace the ones that pop.

Discussion
Following the challenge, sit your team in a circle and ask each member to contribute one thought on the exercise. Obviously, the exercise necessitates working together in close proximity to achieve a common goal. If the team is not close enough, the balloon drops and they must start over. However, if a player gets too close and forcefully invades another's space, the balloon pops and again the team must start over. Use your questions to draw out these messages.

CHAPTER 10

CREDIBLE COACHING

How to Build Your Credibility and Team Chemistry

ESTABLISHING AN EFFECTIVE ENVIRONMENT

As I am sure you have realized by now, successful coaching reaches far beyond your technical ability to teach sports skills and your tactical ability to plan strategy. Successful coaching is also the supreme test of your leadership skills to get a group of individuals headed toward a challenging common goal.

While some of your success depends on your ability to push and pull your players in the right direction, your team has a much better chance of achieving greatness if you can create a conducive climate for success. Your job is to construct a mental, emotional and social environment where the players can come together to maximize the team's potential. When you create a climate engineered for success, you clear a path for the team to make its journey toward greatness.

> *"The coach has a role too: to organize and direct, to create an environment where talent can flourish, to do everything possible to enable the team to win. The major part of my job isn't to tell the players what to do. The most important thing I do is to create a great setting for them to work in."*
> —Coach Pat Riley, Miami Heat

"If you want to build an atmosphere in which everybody pulls together to win, then you, as a leader have to recognize that it all starts with you. It starts with your attitude, your commitment, your caring, your passion for excellence, your dedication to winning. It starts with the example you set. It starts with the way you treat and relate to your players."
—Pat Williams, Senior Executive Vice President, Orlando Magic

MONITORING THE TEAM ENVIRONMENT

As the leader of your team, you have the tremendous responsibility of monitoring how well your team is functioning as a group. It is your job to continually assess and monitor the other Six "C's" of Championship Team Building—your team's goals and performance, your players' commitment, who is accepting their roles, how well you and your players are communicating both on and off the court/field, who is getting along with whom, and whether or not your players respect each other.

Without being conscious of the other Six "C's" as well as possessing the skills and confidence to intervene effectively, your team's ship will be tossed about by the waves of chance, the storms of adversity and the swirling winds of change. What are you to do?

First, help your players recognize and develop the mental and social skills necessary to be an effective team. Just as you would be leery about going into a game without teaching or working on specific sport skills, so too should you be leery when you go into a season without teaching your players how to be a team. Just think of how many problems might be minimized or alleviated if your players knew how to communicate more effectively or learned how to address conflict more constructively. By investing the time to give your players the skills to be an effective team at the beginning of your season, you proactively prevent many problems that could arise.

Secondly, being conscious of the other "C's" is not only important at the beginning, but also must be examined systematically throughout your season. By closely monitoring your team on a regular basis throughout the year, you can catch minor problems and difficulties before they snowball into major crises.

"One of my biggest jobs as a coach is to continually monitor the team for possible brushfires that could occur and to douse them early before they become a raging and damaging inferno."
—Coach Mike Candrea, University of Arizona softball

FIVE STRATEGIES FOR MONITORING YOUR TEAM

1. Coaching Staff

In addition to talking strategy in your weekly coaches' meetings, it's also important to talk about how well your team is functioning. Be sure to check with your coaching staff about any problems or potential conflicts that could arise. Talk about the situation and what each of you may know from a variety of perspectives. By keeping tabs on problems before they occur or while they are still small, you prevent much bigger crises down the road. Assess what might be done about the situation and decide on and implement an appropriate strategy. It might be enough to closely monitor the situation or you may need to have a talk with the player.

2. Captains/Trusted Players

It is critical that you have a good flow of communication between the players on your team. You need to communicate with your captains regularly in an effort to stay in close touch with your team. It's important that you establish an open, honest and trusting relationship with your captains. You have to trust them with a lot of responsibility because they are in a tough position on your team. You have to trust them to honor the confidentiality of their teammates but at the same time believe that they will share information you need to know to effectively lead the team. Often, your captains will adequately address many issues because of their status on the team.

3. Team Council

Some teams create what is called a Team Council. The Council is typically made up of a representative sample of the team which is either selected by the coaches or voted on by the players. Typically at the high school and college level you can select one or two members (depending on the size of your team) from each class (freshmen through senior). You can then have your coaching staff meet with the Council on a weekly or bimonthly basis to discuss the status of the team as well as any areas of concern you or they might be having. Many teams will also utilize the Council to provide input and sometimes decide on disciplinary actions.

4. Entire Team Meetings

Another comprehensive way of monitoring your team is to use your "Pillars of Success" mentioned earlier. You can plan for your team to re-rate your Pillars of Success on a monthly basis. Or you can re-rate the Pillars of Success at strategic times. You may want your team to rate the Pillars when they are playing well so you can build their confidence, reinforce their successes and empower them with the understanding that they have control over their team environment. Conversely, you may want your team to re-rate your Pillars of Success when you're struggling to wake them up and show them what they need to do to get back on track. Team meetings are an opportunity to tap into the team so that you can assess where you are presently and how it positively or negatively affects your chances of reaching your team's mission.

5. Support Staff

Finally, an effective yet sometimes overlooked way to monitor your team is by asking your support staff what they see. Support staff members are often intimately involved with your team and it is amazing what they may know about what is happening. Furthermore, support staff members, while committed to the team, might be able to see situations a bit more objectively and give you more accurate information. If you are fortunate to have a support staff, occasionally check with your strength coach, academic advisors, athletic trainer, and of course, your peak performance consultant (sport psychologist) to obtain their viewpoints.

From my personal experience, one of the first people I will check with when I need to get an update or a more in depth feel for a team is the athletic trainer. They tend to know almost everything that is happening with the team because they hear it from both a player's and coach's perspective. Many athletic trainers are so privy to important team information that I think sport psychology training should be mandatory for them because they often become the unofficial "sport psychologist" of the team.

Of course, as I mentioned with your players, you need to respect your support staff's need to keep certain things confidential. You need to establish an effective relationship with your support staff and trust that they will do what is best for the team. Speaking from practical experience, if you consider them to be covert spies you can pump for information, you put them in an uncomfortable, not to mention unethical position. Rather than interrogating your support staff, it is better to casually ask their perspective and allow them to generally give their opinion about what is going on. Their input will often be enough to clarify the concern or tip you off to what you need to watch or address.

CREDIBILITY IS KING

As outlined in my book *The Seven Secrets of Successful Coaches*, credibility is at the heart of successful coaching. The team must understand your philosophy and have faith that you are the right person to lead the group to the common goal. As you know, coaching is an awesome challenge and responsibility. If your team does not consider you to be a credible coach, it will be very difficult for them to win. Few teams have the ability to win despite their coach. Like cohesion, teams can win despite having less than credible coaches, yet the odds against it are high.

Therefore, it is in your best interest to enhance your credibility not only to bolster your team's chances for success, but probably more so for your own peace of mind. It would be a very sad comment if your players felt that you were an obstacle in the team's success and that they had to overcome your coaching to be successful.

Unfortunately, coaches do not always recognize when they are hurting their team and undermining their own credibility. Like most people, coaches are trying their best to do what they feel is right for the team. It's both a challenge and a risk to put yourself on the line every day. While most coaches definitely mean well, certain decisions and behaviors can have a disastrous effect on the team. Sometimes coaches do not always realize the consequences of their decisions and unwittingly destroy their own credibility as well as disrupt their team chemistry.

15 SUGGESTIONS TO BUILD YOUR CREDIBILITY AND TEAM CHEMISTRY

Let's examine 15 things you can do as a coach that will enhance your credibility and promote your team's chemistry.

1. Attract, recruit and select good people who are team players

Coaches who recruit solely on talent, without regard to the kind of person they are getting, live by the erroneous "talent = success" assumption with which we began our book. They believe that getting the most talented players, regardless of their backgrounds, attitudes or goals, is the key to team success. If you are one of the coaches who still subscribes to this philosophy, please go back to page one and start over.

As I mentioned in the beginning, talent is important. There will be some situations where you may need to recruit a player whose grades are a bit lower than you would like. There are also times when you need to take a minor gamble on a player with a questionable background. However, when you recruit players solely based on talent and not based on character, you start the clock of a ticking time bomb. While it has the potential to bring you short term success, you risk your long term reputation and success on people whom you would probably not trust with your wallet or want your son or daughter to be dating.

Successful coaches consider both talent and character when recruiting and selecting members for their team. They realize that the player needs a high level of sport skills and an acceptable level of personal and social skills for the team to be successful.

To help in player selection, Arizona men's basketball Coach Lute Olson has his current team members spend time with potential recruits so that they can get a feel for the athlete as a person. After the campus visit, Coach Olson discusses the recruit with his current players to get their opinions and to see if the recruit is a good fit with the program.

The players actually get a vote in deciding whether or not to offer the player a scholarship. Involving your players in recruiting helps to ensure the health of your program and has the additional benefit of showing your players that you value their input on decisions which affect the entire team.

> *"To be successful, a team must have the highest caliber people, and they must be able to operate in sync, in harmony, in balance."*
> —Pat Williams, Senior Executive Vice President, Orlando Magic

2. Show concern for players as people

Coaches create big problems when they overlook the personal lives of their players. Leaders are successful because of two main qualities—their concern for productivity and their concern for people. While many coaches do a great job of emphasizing the task and reaching the goal (productivity), the best coaches are the ones who match their emphasis on winning with an equal, and perhaps greater emphasis on developing successful people.

Remember, your players are not just athletes but people. They play many roles in their lives such as student, child, sibling, friend, parent, etc. Some of these roles are as important, and yes, more important than their athletic role. As a coach it is important for you to value and respect the other roles a person wants and needs to play. Sometimes coaches get so caught up in seeing their players only as "athletes" that they forget to ask about their other interests. Remember that your players often have concerns about their families, friends and futures outside of the sports world. It's critical that you take an interest in the person who happens to be an athlete rather than just interacting with them solely as an athlete.

Be sure to give them as much praise for getting an "A" on a test as you do when they make the game winning play. Also, be there for them when obstacles occur in their personal lives such as a breakup with a boy/girlfriend or a death in the family. When you respect your athletes as people, they will know that you care about them and be willing to "spill their guts" for you.

> *"People don't care how much you know until they know how much you care."*
> —Coaching Principle

"It doesn't matter whether you are in football, real estate, or electronics, the people who work for you will be happier and more productive if they feel they have value to you beyond what they can do for you on the job. The want to feel that they are important on a personal level.
—Coach Marty Schottenheimer, San Diego Chargers

3. Build a trusting relationship with your players

Just as you need to be able to trust your players to run a successful program, so too do your players need to trust you. As I mentioned in an earlier chapter, trust is built when people do what they say they will do. Your players need to be able to trust you and take what you say to them at face value.

Coaches who are less than completely honest with their players are setting themselves up for some major damage. While you might be able to pacify a player for a short time by insinuating more playing time is right around the corner, it will be a bigger problem for you and the entire team if you did not mean it. You owe it to your players to be honest with them, even if it could hurt their feelings. When you continually lead players on with the hope of playing time yet in reality know they won't play, you manipulate their hopes and dreams. When other players see that you are willing to do it to one of their teammates, it is logical for them to think that you could also treat them the same way. Trust takes a long time to build and can be destroyed in a second.

4. Want success for your players and give them credit

Obviously as a coach you want to be successful and you play a key role in helping your team win. Big problems can occur though when you take all the credit for the win. Unfortunately, there are some coaches out there who are too ego-involved. They coach and compete solely to make themselves look good. They look to get all the glory and praise when their team does well and perhaps place too much importance on their role. You can easily identify these coaches because they tend to credit good coaching when their team wins and blame the players when they lose. By not appreciating the players who actually perform on the field, these coaches undermine their team's success by hogging all of the glory. They tend to talk about their own accomplishments rather than about their players' successes.

Good coaches give credit to their players for their wins. They realize that their players are the ones who play the game. By giving them credit, it empowers their players and builds their confidence for future games. While successful coaches do receive a sense of self-satisfaction when their team does well, they are more interested in coaching the team for the players' success and helping them achieve their goals. Good coaches also are willing to shoulder the responsibility for some losses to take pressure off the team.

5. Stay in touch with your team

When a coach does not have a close connection with her team, or doesn't understand her player's goals, frustrations, concerns and conflicts, she misses problems that are likely eroding the cohesion of her team. Believe it or not, I know some coaches who basically show up at practice time, make sure the players are in the right spots of the X's and O's that the coach has diagramed, and then head home right after practice. They take a very strategically calculated but emotionally sterile approach to the team. This style can be somewhat effective if you are a master tactician of your sport, but be careful when you neglect the personal and social aspects of your team. Neglecting the relationships on your team is like ignoring a five year old playing with matches. In both situations, someone is likely to end up getting burned. Furthermore, you're missing the performance enhancing effect of solid teamwork to propel your team to higher levels.

Like good doctors, successful coaches continually monitor the vital signs of their teams. They know which players are struggling with their roles, which players aren't getting along with their teammates, and they know when the team needs to be pushed and when to draw back. By being in touch with the team's natural ebbs and flows, these coaches can better plan practices and appropriately influence and intervene when necessary.

6. Avoid coddling your superstars or negative players

A sure way to hurt your team is when you let your superstars or negative players run the show. Amazingly, while the coach should be the person in control, sometimes it's actually a certain player who knows how to manipulate the coach that calls all the shots.

Some coaches abdicate their responsibility to their players, especially their superstars, because they are afraid of upsetting them or even losing them to a different team. One of the toughest situations to handle for most coaches is when a superstar breaks the team's standards. You have a choice between coddling or confronting your superstar. Unfortunately, too many coaches go the coddling route, giving in to their superstar and giving up their credibility and team chemistry. It's almost as if they are held hostage by the whims of terrorist type players, some of whom are less than 18 years old! The resentment created among other teammates when you coddle a player has devastating and demoralizing effects. While you might be able to save your superstar, you end up losing the respect of the rest of your team.

> *"A common mistake made by some coaches*
> *is they let their superstars write their own rules."*
> —Coach Dennis Green, Minnesota Vikings

7. Be dedicated and know your stuff

Coaches also lose credibility when they do not have the desire and commitment to be successful. It's hard to demand that your players work hard when they know you don't invest the time to plan a practice, when you're not willing to come early or stay late to help them with their game, or when you leave the office early every day to play golf or relax. You need to demand as much of yourself as you do from your players to earn and maintain your credibility in their eyes.

8. Create a cohesive coaching staff

One of the most hypocritical situations that undermines a coach's credibility and a team's success is when the coaching staff is not cohesive. The same Seven "C's" that apply to your overall team definitely apply to the smaller group of your coaching staff. You can't preach teamwork to your players when they see that you and your staff can't get along. I'm amazed when coaches criticize their fellow staff members in front of their own players. It's one thing to recognize some shortcomings of another coach when talking with a player but it is a whole other thing to bad mouth the coach.

Thus, head coaches need to find assistants who can complement their skills and be loyal to them. Make sure that if your assistants have a problem with something you are doing they go directly to you, behind closed doors, to discuss the situation. I have seen some coaches argue back and forth and actually get into a punch-throwing fight in front of the team. You're not always going to agree with each other, but you need to agree that you will do your disagreeing behind closed doors away from the team.

Assistant coaches should be sure they understand what they are getting into before accepting a position on the staff. While you and the head coach do not always need to think alike, you must make sure that your basic coaching values and philosophies are compatible. If you are uncomfortable with something, make sure you discuss it with your head coach as soon as possible. Furthermore, if you are in a situation where you do not fit well with the head coach and know that not much is going to change, then it's probably time to move on.

> *"If you asked me what is the most important factor*
> *in whatever success Wake Forest has had I would say*
> *it's staff chemistry and our ability as a staff to work*
> *cohesively and complement each other."*
> —Coach David Odom, University of South Carolina men's basketball

9. Define and appreciate roles

With complementary roles being one of the Seven "C's" of Championship Team Building, coaches hurt the team when they do not clearly define roles for their players. All too frequently, athletes come into my office because they are confused about their role on the team. Players need to know where they stand with you so they can clarify their own expectations as well as tailor their training. Players want to know how they fit into the team and if you don't tell them, they frequently jump to the wrong assumptions and conclusions.

Further, as we discussed the importance of coaches and teammates appreciating everyone's role, another problem occurs when coaches only give feedback and appreciation to the starters, while ignoring the reserves. I know one coach who treats his starters like kings and treats his subs like dirt. While it might be a good incentive to work hard for some to attain the "king" status, the rest of the players basically lose motivation because they receive no coaching. The situation becomes very interesting when an injury occurs on the team. The coach now needs to rely on a player off the "Dirt Squad" who often has little confidence and rusty skills because he was hardly ever coached. This coach ends up hurting his team in the long run because he never spends time developing his reserves, much less appreciating them.

Successful coaches invest the time to clearly communicate each player's role. While it may disappoint some players to know that they will be on the bench, the honest communication helps them set their expectations and understand the areas they need to improve to have a chance to break into the lineup. Also, successful coaches may spend more time with their starting unit, but not at the emotional expense of their reserves. They look to acknowledge and praise each player's contribution, no matter how large or small it might be. By defining and appreciating everyone's role, coaches help to create a conducive climate for team success.

10. Be consistent

Coaches who are inconsistent either in their moods or strategies can hurt their team. Consistency is an important tenant of raising emotionally stable children and is equally important in coaching. Inconsistent coaches end up confusing their players because they are never sure what is and is not acceptable. One minute you might be joking around with your players and the next minute you are yelling at them because they are not taking the game seriously. Or early in the season you practice one strategy and then mysteriously in the middle of the season you abandon it and start with a completely different one. Inconsistent coaches and inconsistent coaching makes it difficult for players to feel comfortable.

Successful coaches stay consistent with their philosophies, standards and strategies. This is not to say that you can't make modifications or improvements every now and then, but basically your players should know what to expect from you during games and practices.

*"To be credible, you must be consistent. Any sign
of inconsistency, you lose credibility instantly."*
—Coach Pat Summitt, University of Tennessee women's basketball

*"Consistency is vital in the way you respond to people's
performance. I pride myself in the fact that our players
can count on our coaching staff to be consistently
observing and responding in a consistent manner."*
—Coach Don Shula, Miami Dolphins

11. Know when to let up, have fun and avoid burnout

Coaches who have a tendency to be more "obsessed" on the commitment continuum can drive their players too hard. While hard work and commitment are vital to the success of your team, there are times when you need to ease up on your players. Remember, there is such a thing as a recovery cycle. Human beings can work hard and accomplish some amazing things but we also need a break physically as well as mentally every now and then. Seasons span many months and in order to have a team that can reach the Performing stage and peak at the end of the season, you need to make sure that they have enough left to give it their all.

Good coaches sense when they need to push their players and when they might need to ease up a bit. Many coaches will work their teams long and hard in the early season, focusing on the quantity of repetitions to develop their players skills and stamina. As the end of the season draws near, they shorten their practices focusing more on concentrated, quality workouts. Be sure your players are working hard enough to earn confidence in their abilities, but not too hard that you drive the motivation and fun completely out of them. If your "committed" and "compelled" players are starting to become burned out, you probably need to back off a bit.

12. Avoid excessive competition within the team

While competition is definitely necessary and often healthy within your team, sometimes coaches go overboard and set up an unhealthy, cutthroat environment. Healthy competition promotes players to work hard, handle pressure and perform at their best as they compete for spots. You should encourage your players to battle on the field but be teammates off the field. Sometimes coaches take competition for spots too far and players try to criticize, undermine and even injure each other in an attempt to come out ahead. Encourage your players to respect their teammates, especially the ones they are competing against. For it's these players who push everyone to get better, which in the long run helps the team.

13. Be a positive role model

Preaching one thing and practicing another destroys your credibility. You can't tell your players to stay in control when they get bad calls while you continually go ballistic and berate officials. Your players will take their cues from how you act in a variety of situations. Successful coaches understand that they set the tone for their teams and need to constantly model the type of behavior they expect and demand from their players, both on and off the court.

14. Establish a mission as well as the process of attaining it

Many coaches do a good job of establishing a mission for the season. The typical problem though is they don't do a good enough job getting their players to focus on the process of achieving it. As I stressed in the beginning chapters, your team needs to establish a mission to work toward. This process helps to clarify your team's purpose for all the long hours you will put in throughout the season. After determining your mission, you need to get your players focusing on the little steps that will maximize your chances of reaching it. Successful coaches get their players to take care of the process of being successful by talking about it often and rewarding their players based more on the process than the outcome.

15. Involve your players and hold them accountable

Finally, remember to involve your players in the decisions that affect your team as much as possible. The autocratic style of coaching, while prominent many years ago, has become very difficult to use with today's athlete. You will find it tough to run your team like a drill sergeant anymore because most people are not going to respond to that kind of coaching. Instead, you need to show your players that you respect their opinions and are willing to consider them as you coach. Of course this doesn't mean that you are going to do whatever your players want, but it does mean that you are open enough to solicit and value their input.

When you involve your players and give them the power to have input on the team, you need to hold them accountable for their decisions. You also need to hold them accountable for their attitudes, effort and teamwork on a daily basis so that they can follow through on the commitment necessary to achieve their goals.

Credibility is Fragile: Handle With Care

One of the toughest rules about enhancing your credibility is that it takes a long time to build but can be destroyed in a second. When properly built and manintained, your credibility with your players as a competent and caring leader will give you the power to create a constructive environment where your players can develop to their fullest potential.

CHAPTER TEN SUMMARY
TEAM BUILDING TIPS

- Your role as a coach is to create an effective team environment.
- Credible coaching means you have a good feel for what is going on with your team.
- Involve your coaching staff, players and support staff to help you monitor your team.
- Coach in ways that build team chemistry and avoid unintentionally undermining it.
- Recruit and select good people who are team players.
- Show your players that you sincerely care about them as people.
- Make sure you are coaching your players instead of coddling them.
- Credibility takes a long time to build but can be instantly destroyed.

CHAPTER 11

SUMMARY

It's Time to Set Sail

As the captain of your team's ship, it is now time for you and your crew to sail the Seven "C's" of Championship Team Building. By carefully selecting your crew and involving them in determining your mission and charting your course, you now have a clear picture of your desired destination, as well as the potential rewards and treasures that await you. Because you value the goals and insights or your crew, you can count on their commitment to give it their best effort. You assign each of your crew members an important role that will help the team achieve its mission and you let them know how much you appreciate each of their contributions. You clearly communicate with your crew and prepare them to constructively weather the inevitable storms of conflict and adversity. With their common goal in mind, your crew feels a sense of kinship and cohesiveness. Finally, as the captain of the ship, you respect and care about your crew which effectively guards against any chance of mutiny.

Team Building Answers, Strategies & Solutions

My mission in writing this book was to provide you with a practical and proven resource to help you effectively address and answer many of the common and complex questions coaches have involving team building. For us to effectively evaluate whether the time and money you invested in this book was worth your while, I invite you to take another look at the questions listed at the beginning:

How can I get my team to be just half as committed to success as I am?

How do I get everyone on the same page and focused on a common goal?

How do I convince my players to work together as a team?

How do I handle selfish players who have their own agendas?

How do I get my players to understand, appreciate and accept their roles?

How do I get my players to communicate better both on and off the court/field?

What can I do when my team has problems and can't get along with each other?

How can I get my players to be more responsible and accountable?

How can I get my team to respect and trust each other more?

If you recall, these questions are the same issues and problems that may have puzzled and plagued many of you and your fellow coaches in the past. By investing your time to read about the theories, suggestions, quotes and practical experiences contained in this book, my hope and belief is that you have acquired many ideas, strategies and solutions to effectively answer each of the questions.

Continuing Education

Coaching is a process of continuous learning. If you enjoyed this book and found it helpful, I strongly recommend that you check out the other books listed in the Recommended Readings section. I really appreciate the chance to share some of my experiences and observations with you and invite you do the same for me. I encourage you to contact me via phone—1-888-721-TEAM or e-mail—jeff@jeffjanssen.com to share your personal team building innovations, frustrations and celebrations. Together we can always learn more about what it takes to build a championship team.

As we come to the conclusion of this book, I sincerely hope you achieved your goal of learning more about what you can do as a coach to build a motivated, committed and cohesive team. Championship team building is truly one of the most complex and challenging responsibilities of coaching. However, the potential rewards of greater success and satisfaction for you and your players far outweigh the costs. Regardless of your team's talent, by investing the time in team building, you give yourself and your team that extra edge which could make the difference in winning a championship. More importantly, you also give your players the necessary skills to be an effective team player so they can leave a lasting legacy on the game of life.

RECOMMENDED READINGS

Coach's and Sports Books

Barnett, Gary & Gregorian, Vahe, *High Hopes,* Warner Books, New York: 1996.

Blanchard, Ken & Shula, Don, *Everyone's a Coach,* Harper Business, New York: 1995.

Bowden, Bobby, Bowden, Terry & Brown, Ben, *Winning's Only Part of the Game,* Warner Books, New York: 1996.

Brill, William & Krzyzewski, Mike, *A Season is a Lifetime,* Simon & Schuster, New York: 1993.

Didenger, Ray, *Game Plans for Success,* Contemporary Books, Chicago: 1995.

Jackson, Phil & Delehanty, Hugh, *Sacred Hoops,* Hyperion, New York: 1995.

Janssen, Jeff & Candrea, Mike, *Mental Training for Softball,* Southwest Camps Publications, Casa Grande, AZ: 1998.

Jordan, Michael, I *Can't Accept Not Trying,* HarperCollins, New York: 1994.

Jordan, Michael, *Rare Air,* HarperCollins, New York: 1993.

Martens, Rainer, *Coaches Guide to Sport Psychology,* Human Kinetics, Champaign, IL: 1987.

Odom, David, *The End is Not the Trophy,* Carolina Academic Press, Durham, NC: 1998.

Pitino, Rick & Reynolds, Bill, *Success is a Choice,* Broadway Books, New York: 1997.

Riley, Pat, *The Winner Within,* Putnam, New York: 1993.

Summitt, Pat & Jenkins, Sally, *Reach for the Summit,* Broadway Books, New York: 1998.

Telander, Rick, *In the Year of the Bull,* Simon & Schuster, New York: 1996.

Tomjanovich, Rudy & Falkoff, Robert, *A Rocket at Heart,* Simon & Schuster, New York: 1997.

Vernacchia, Ralph, McGuire, Richard & Cook, David, *Coaching Mental Excellence,* Brown & Benchmark, Dubuque, IA: 1992.

Warren, William, *Coaching and Control,* Prentice Hall, Paramus, NJ: 1997.

Warren, William, *Coaching and Motivation,* Prentice Hall, Paramus, NJ: 1983.

Williams, Pat, *The Magic of Teamwork,* Thomas Nelson Publishers, Nashville, TN: 1997.

Williams, Pat, *Go for the Magic,* Thomas Nelson Publishers, Nashville, TN: 1995.

Wooden, John, *They Call Me Coach,* Contemporary Books, Chicago: 1988.

Yukelson, David, Principles of Effective Team Building Interventions in Sport: A Direct Services Approach at Penn State University, *Journal of Applied Sport Psychology, 9,* 73-96.

Books with Experiential Exercises and Team Building Games

Newstrom, John & Scannell, Edward, *The Big Book of Team Building Games,* McGraw-Hill, New York: 1998.

Newstrom, John & Scannell, Edward, *The Big Book of Business Games,* McGraw-Hill, New York: 1996.

Rohnke, Karl & Butler, Steve, *Quicksilver,* Kendall/Hunt Publishing, Dubuque, IA: 1995.

Rohnke, Karl, *Cowtails and Cobras II,* Kendall/Hunt Publishing, Dubuque, IA: 1989.

Rohnke, Karl, *Silver Bullets,* Kendall/Hunt Publishing, Dubuque, IA: 1984.

Scannell, Edward & Newstrom, John, *The Big Book of Presentation Games,* McGraw-Hill, New York: 1998.

Scannell, Edward & Newstrom, John, *The Complete Games Trainers Play,* McGraw-Hill, New York: 1994.

Business Books for Team Building

Covey, Stephen, *Principle-Centered Leadership*, Simon & Schuster, New York: 1991.

Covey, Stephen, *The Seven Habits of Highly Effective People*, Simon & Schuster, New York: 1989.

Katzenberg, Jon & Smith, Douglas, *The Wisdom of Teams*, HarperBusiness, New York, 1993.

Kouzes, James & Posner, Barry, *Credibility*, Jossey-Bass, San Francisco: 1993.

Kouzes, James & Posner, Barry, *The Leadership Challenge*, Jossey-Bass, San Francisco: 1987.

Quick, Thomas, *Successful Team Building*, American Management Association, New York: 1992.

Schultz, Howard, *Pour Your Heart into It*, Hyperion, New York: 1997.

ABOUT THE AUTHOR

As one the nation's premiere Peak Performance Coaches, Jeff Janssen, M.S. helps coaches and athletes develop the team chemisty, mental toughness, and leadership skills necessary to win championships.

As a speaker and consultant to many of the nation's top colleges including North Carolina, Michigan, Stanford, Tennessee, Florida, Florida State, Wisconsin, LSU, NC State, Maryland, Alabama, and Arizona, Janssen's work has contributed to numerous NCAA National Championships and Final Fours across a variety of sports.

Jeff is the co-developer and lead instructor in the world-renowned Carolina Leadership Academy, widely considered the top leadership development program in collegiate athletics. The cutting edge Carolina Leadership Academy develops, challenges, and supports University of North Carolina student-athletes, coaches and staff in their continual quest to become world-class leaders.

In addition to the sporting world, Jeff speaks to and consults with Fortune 500 companies including Federal Express, Raytheon, and New York Life. Janssen's interactive and inspiring workshops provide businesses with the important mental edge in the highly competitive corporate arena.

A prolific writer, Janssen has written and produced numerous articles, books, audios, and videos on peak performance, team building, and credible coaching. His groundbreaking books *Championship Team Building, The Team Captain's Leadership Manual,* and *The Seven Secrets of Successful Coaches* have received rave reviews from coaches and business managers alike.

Jeff resides in the Raleigh/Durham area in Cary, North Carolina with his wife Kristi, son Ryan, and daughter Jill. They enjoy family outings, great restaurants, reading, and playing and watching all kinds of sports.

Peak Performance Presentations

Jeff Janssen offers a variety Peak Performance Presentations for coaches and athletes of all sports and levels designed to help individuals and teams perform to their potential.

CHAMPIONSHIP TEAM BUILDING WORKSHOP

Based on the popular book, *Championship Team Building,* this customized workshop gives your team the insights and strategies necessary to develop great team chemistry. The fun and fast paced workshop uses several team building games, challenges and exercises to reveal the strengths and weaknesses of your team. Determine a common and compelling goal, build a lasting commitment, define and appreciate roles, minimize and manage conflict and create a more cohesive team. Half and full day programs available.

SECRETS OF SPORT PSYCHOLOGY SEMINAR

This innovative and interactive seminar shows athletes and coaches how to Master The Mental Game for sport success. Learn how to develop the same peak performance mindset as Olympic and National Championship athletes and coaches. You and your team will learn how to effectively build your confidence, sharpen your focus, perform under pressure, trust your talents and overcome obstacles and adversity. Hundreds of professional, collegiate and high school teams across the nation have gained the mental advantage through this powerful and inspiring seminar. You can even use it as fund-raiser for your team or entire athletic department.

SEVEN SECRETS OF SUCCESSFUL COACHES WORKSHOP

This coaches' development workshop examines the seven secrets of successful coaches and gives you the skills to become a more respected, effective, and credible coach. Learn how to communicate more effectively with your athletes, build their confidence and commitment, handle difficult players and discipline, motivate and inspire your team, earn your athletes' respect, and leave a meaningful and lasting legacy as a coach. Discover how to coach, communicate, and connect with today's athletes. Makes an ideal continuing education program for your college or high school athletic department coaching staff.

DEVELOPING EFFECTIVE TEAM LEADERS WORKSHOP

This leadership workshop is ideal for college and high school athletic departments who want to develop dynamic, responsible, and effective leaders both in sport and the game of life. Create leaders who will set and maintain high standards, promote a respectful, responsible, and accountable environment, combat negativity and complacency, constructively confront undisciplined teammates, and keep your team focused when adversity strikes. Help your program develop the positive and powerful leaders it needs to succeed.

A partial list of Jeff's satisfied clients:

Stanford University, University of Florida, University of Tennessee, University of Wisconsin, University of Texas, University of Alabama, DePaul University, Florida State University, Xavier University, Federal Express, Raytheon, New York Life, 1st National Reserve, Little Chute High School, Douglas County High School, Dakota Ridge High School...

For additional information about Jeff Janssen's
Peak Performance Presentations you can contact him at:

  Phone: 1-888-721-TEAM (toll free)
  Email: jeff@jeffjanssen.com
  Website: www.jeffjanssen.com

Peak Performance Products

Jeff Janssen has produced several educational resources on team building, peak performance, and leadership.

Books

THE TEAM CAPTAIN'S LEADERSHIP MANUAL $29.95
The Complete Guide to Developing Team Leaders
Whom Coaches Respect and Teammates Trust

CHAMPIONSHIP TEAM BUILDING $29.95
What Every Coach Needs to Know to Build a
Motivated, Committed & Cohesive Team

THE SEVEN SECRETS OF SUCCESSFUL COACHES $29.95
How to Unlock and Unleash Your Team's Full Potential

JEFF JANSSEN'S PEAK PERFORMANCE PLAYBOOK $24.95
50 Drills, Activities & Ideas to Inspire Your Team
Build Mental Toughness & Improve Team Chemistry

THE MENTAL MAKINGS OF CHAMPIONS $19.95
How to Win The Mental Game

Videos

WINNING THE MENTAL GAME $29.95
How You Can Develop the Motivation,
Confidence & Focus of Champions

PSYCHOLOGY OF SENSATIONAL HITTING $39.95
How You Can Be A More Focused, Confident & Consistent
Hitter with Olympic Gold Medalist Leah O'Brien

BUILDING A WINNING TEAM CHEMISTRY $29.95

Audio

THE SOFTBALL COACH'S GUIDE TO
MENTAL TRAINING $39.95
with Sport Psych Consultant Ken Ravizza

To learn more about these resources or to place an order
call toll free **1-888-721-TEAM**
or visit **www.jeffjanssen.com**

All Major Credit Cards and Purchase Orders Accepted

NOTES

Quotes from the listed people came from the following sources:

Coach Gary Barnett, Colorado Football
Barnett, Gary & Gregorian, Vahe, *High Hopes*, Warner Books, New
York: 1996.

Coach Don Shula, Miami Dolphins
Blanchard, Ken & Shula, Don, *Everyone's a Coach*, Harper Business,
New York: 1995.

Coach Mike Krzyzewski, Duke University men's basketball
Brill, William & Krzyzewski, Mike, *A Season is a Lifetime*, Simon &
Schuster, New York: 1993.

Coach Dennis Green, Minnesota Vikings
Didenger, Ray, *Game Plans for Success*, Contemporary Books,
Chicago: 1995.

Coach Marty Schottenheimer, San Diego Chargers
Didenger, Ray, *Game Plans for Success*, Contemporary Books,
Chicago: 1995.

Coach Phil Jackson, Los Angeles Lakers
Jackson, Phil & Delehanty, Hugh, *Sacred Hoops*, Hyperion, New
York: 1995.

Michael Jordan, Chicago Bulls/Washington Wizards
Jordan, Michael, *I Can't Accept Not Trying*, HarperCollins, New
York: 1994.

Coach Dave Odom, University of South Carolina men's basketball
Odom, David, *The End is Not the Trophy*, Carolina Academic Press,
Durham, NC: 1998.

Coach Rick Pitino, University of Louisville men's basketball
Pitino, Rick & Reynolds, Bill, *Success is a Choice*, Broadway Books,
New York: 1997.

Coach Pat Riley, Miami Heat
Riley, Pat, *The Winner Within*, Putnam, New York: 1993.

Coach Pat Summitt, University of Tennessee women's basketball
Summitt, Pat & Jenkins, Sally, *Reach for the Summit*, Broadway
    Books, New York: 1998.

Pat Williams, Senior Executive Vice President, Orlando Magic
Williams, Pat, *The Magic of Teamwork*, Thomas Nelson Publishers,
    Nashville, TN: 1997.

Coach John Wooden, UCLA men's basketball
Wooden, John, *They Call Me Coach*, Contemporary Books, Chicago:
    1988.

Coach Bill Walsh, San Francisco 49ers
Walsh, Bill and Dickey, Glenn, *Building a Champion*, St. Martin's
    Paperbacks, New York: 1990.

Howard Schultz, CEO Starbucks Coffee
Schultz, Howard, *Pour Your Heart into It*, Hyperion, New York: 1997.

Coach Rudy Tomjanovich, Houston Rockets
Tomjanovich, Rudy & Falkoff, Robert, *A Rocket at Heart*, Simon &
    Schuster, New York: 1997.

Stephen Covey
Covey, Stephen, *The Seven Habits of Highly Effective People*, Simon
    & Schuster, New York: 1989.

Photo credits

Cover Photo Credits: Arizona Daily Star & University of Arizona Photo Center.
Interior Photo Credits: University Photo Center (pp. vii, xviii, 4, 34, 108),
University of Arizona Media Relations (pp. 12, 54, 134, 152, 168),
Northwestern Athletics (pp. 122, 172),
Peter H. Bick (p. 92),
Leah Zucker (p. 70),
Monica Armenta & Steph Sammaritano (p. 176)
Jeff Janssen (p. viii).

Index

To order additional copies of

CHAMPIONSHIP
TEAM BUILDING

*What Every Coach Needs to Know to Build a
Motivated, Committed & Cohesive Team*

Call toll free 1-888-721-TEAM

Fax: (919) 303-4338

On-line: www.jeffjanssen.com

Mail: Winning The Mental Game
       102 Horne Creek Court
       Cary, NC 27519

All major credit cards are accepted.

Shipping: $5.00 for the first item, $1.00 for each additional item.

NC tax: Add 7% sales tax for orders shipped to NC addresses.

Call for information on volume discounts to groups and associations.

Satisfaction guaranteed or your money back!

- -

Championship Team Building Order Form

Name_____

Sport/Team_____

Address_____

City, State, Zip_____

Phone_____

E-mail_____

Credit Card#_____

Expiration_____